SOUPS &
STARTERS

SOUPS & STARTERS

SIMPLY SENSATIONAL DISHES FOR EVERY
MEAL AND ANY OCCASION

Linda Fraser

TED SMART

This edition produced for The Book People Ltd
Hall Wood Avenue, Haydock, St Helens. WA11 9UL

© Anness Publishing Limited 1999, 2002

Anness Publishing Limited, Hermes House, 88–89 Blackfriars Road, London SE1 8HA

Published in the USA by Anness Publishing Inc. 27 West 20th Street, New York, NY 10011

A CIP catalogue record for this book is available from the British Library.

Publisher: Joanna Lorenz
Senior Cookery Editor: Linda Fraser
Designers: Tony Paine and Roy Prescott
Photographers: Steve Baxter, Karl Adamson and Amanda Heywood
Food for Photography: Wendy Lee, Jane Stevenson and Elizabeth Wolf-Cohen
Props Stylists: Blake Minton and Kirsty Rawlings
Additional recipes: Carla Capalbo and Laura Washburn
Production Controller: Joanna King

1 3 5 7 9 10 8 6 4 2

Front cover shows French Onion Soup, for recipe see page 20

Previously published as *Soups & Starters*

ACKNOWLEDGEMENTS
For their assistance in the publication of this book, the publishers wish to thank:

Kenwood Appliances plc
New Lane
Havant
Hants PO9 2NH

Magimix
115A High Street
Godalming, Surrey
GU7 1AQ

Prestige
Prestige House
22–26 High Street
Egham
Surrey
TW20 9DU

Le Creuset
The Kitchenware Merchants Ltd
4 Stephenson Close
East Portway
Andover
Hampshire SP10 3RU

The apple symbol indicates a low fat, low cholesterol recipe.

NOTES
Bracketed terms are intended for American readers.
For all recipes, quantities are given in both metric and imperial measures and, where appropriate, measures are also given
in standard cups and spoons. Follow one set, but not a mixture, because they are not interchangeable.
Standard spoon and cup measures are level. 1 tsp = 5ml, 1 tbsp = 15ml, 1 cup = 250ml/8fl oz
Australian standard tablespoons are 20ml. Australian readers should use 3 tsp in place of 1 tbsp for measuring
small quantities of gelatine, flour, salt, etc.
Medium (US large) eggs are used unless otherwise stated.

CONTENTS

STOCKS FOR SOUPS

There's no doubt that the best soups are based on home-made stock, and although stocks can be time-consuming to make, their superior flavour makes all the effort worthwhile. Stock can of course be prepared ahead, when you have the time to cook and the ingredients on hand – some stocks will keep for up to four or five days in the fridge, and for as long as six months in the freezer. There are four main types of stock: fish, vegetable, meat and poultry, and here we guide you through the techniques and processes, step-by-step. Vegetable and fish stocks are quickest to prepare as they only need simmering for about half an hour.

MAKING FISH STOCK

Fish stock is much quicker to make than meat or poultry stock. Ask your fishmonger for heads, bones and trimmings from white fish.

Makes about 1 litre/2 pints

700g/1½lb heads, bones and trimmings
   from white fish
1 onion, sliced
2 celery sticks with leaves, chopped
1 carrot, sliced
½ lemon, sliced (optional)
1 bay leaf
a few fresh parsley sprigs
6 black peppercorns
1.35 litres/2¼ pints water
150ml/¼ pint dry white wine

1 Rinse the fish heads, bones and trimmings well under cold running water. Put in a stockpot with the vegetables, lemon, if using, the herbs, peppercorns, water and wine. Bring to the boil, skimming the surface frequently, then reduce the heat and simmer for 25 minutes.

2 Strain the stock without pressing down on the ingredients in the sieve. If not using immediately, leave to cool and then chill. Fish stock should be used within 2 days, or it can be frozen for up to 3 months.

MAKING VEGETABLE STOCK

Vary the ingredients for this fresh-flavoured stock according to what you have to hand. Chill, covered, for up to 5 days; freeze up to 1 month.

Makes about 2.5 litres/4 pints

2 large onions, coarsely chopped
2 leeks, sliced
3 garlic cloves, crushed with the flat
   side of a knife
3 carrots, coarsely chopped
4 celery sticks, coarsely chopped
a large strip of lemon rind
a handful of parsley stalks (about 12)
a few fresh thyme sprigs
2 bay leaves
2.5 litres/4 pints water

1 Put the vegetables, lemon rind, herbs and water in a stockpot and bring to the boil. Skim off the foam that rises to the surface, frequently at first and then from time to time.

2 Reduce the heat and simmer, uncovered, for 30 minutes. Strain the stock and leave it to cool.

MAKING POULTRY STOCK

A good home-made poultry stock is invaluable in the kitchen. It is simple and economical to make, and can be stored in the freezer for up to six months. If poultry giblets are available, add them to the stockpot (except the livers) with the wings.

Makes about 2.5 litres/4 pints

1.12–1.35kg/2½–3lb poultry wings, backs and necks (chicken, turkey, etc)
2 onions, unpeeled and quartered
4 litres/6½ pints cold water
2 carrots, roughly chopped
2 celery stalks, with leaves if possible, roughly chopped
a small handful of fresh parsley
a few fresh thyme sprigs or 5ml/1tsp dried thyme
1 or 2 bay leaves
10 black peppercorns, lightly crushed

A FRUGAL STOCK

Stock can be made from the bones and carcasses of roasted poultry, cooked with vegetables and flavourings. Save the carcasses in a polythene bag in the freezer until you have three or four, then make stock. It may not have quite as rich a flavour as stock made from a whole bird or fresh wings, backs and necks, but it will still taste fresher and less salty than stock made from a cube.

1 Combine the poultry wings, backs and necks and the onions in a stockpot. Cook over moderate heat, stirring occasionally so they colour evenly, until lightly browned.

3 Add the remaining ingredients. Partly cover the stockpot and gently simmer the stock for 3 hours.

5 When cold, remove the layer of fat that will have set on the surface.

2 Add the water and stir well to mix in the sediment on the bottom of the pot. Bring to the boil and skim off the impurities as they rise to the surface of the stock.

4 Strain the stock into a bowl and leave to cool, then refrigerate.

STOCK TIPS

If wished, use a whole bird for making stock instead of wings, backs and necks. A boiling fowl will give a wonderful flavour and provide plenty of chicken meat to use in soups and casseroles.

No salt is added to stock because as the stock reduces the flavour becomes concentrated and saltiness increases. Add salt to the dish in which the stock is used.

MAKING MEAT STOCK

The most delicious meat soups rely on a good home-made stock for success. Neither a stock cube nor a canned consommé will do if you want the best flavour. Once made, meat stock can be kept in the refrigerator for four or five days, or frozen for longer storage (up to six months).

ON THE LIGHT SIDE

For a light meat stock, use veal bones and do not roast the bones or vegetables. Put in the pot with cold water and cook as described.

Makes about 2 litres / 3¹/₂ pints

1.8kg/4lb beef bones, such as shin, leg and neck, or veal or lamb bones, cut into 6cm/2½in pieces
2 onions, unpeeled, quartered
2 carrots, roughly chopped
2 celery sticks, with leaves if possible, roughly chopped
2 tomatoes, coarsely chopped
4.5 litres/7½ pints cold water
a handful of parsley stalks
a few fresh thyme sprigs or 5ml/1 tsp dried thyme
2 bay leaves
10 black peppercorns, lightly crushed

1 Preheat the oven to 230°C/450°F/ Gas 8. Put the bones in a roasting tin or flameproof casserole and roast, turning occasionally, for 30 minutes or until they start to brown.

2 Add the onions, carrots, celery and tomatoes and baste with the fat in the tin. Roast for a further 20-30 minutes or until the bones are well browned. Stir and baste occasionally.

3 Transfer the bones and vegetables to a stockpot. Spoon off the fat from the roasting tin or casserole.

4 Add a little of the water to the roasting tin or casserole and bring to the boil on top of the stove, stirring well to scrape up any browned bits. Pour this liquid into the stockpot.

5 Add the remaining water. Bring just to the boil, skimming frequently to remove all the foam from the surface. Add the parsley, thyme, bay leaves and peppercorns.

6 Partly cover the pot and simmer the stock for 4–6 hours. The bones and vegetables should always be covered with liquid, so top up with a little boiling water from time to time if necessary.

7 Strain the stock through a sieve. Skim as much fat as possible from the surface. If possible, cool the stock and then chill it; the fat will rise to the top and set in a layer that can be removed easily.

PREPARING STARTERS

Starters are usually served at the beginning of special meals, or when you are entertaining, so they need either to be easy to put together at the last minute, or able to be prepared ahead. The recipe sections include all sorts of hot and cold starters, and here we give you some special techniques: from making perfect mayonnaise and vinaigrette dressing, to preparing, cooking – and eating – a globe artichoke. You'll also discover just how easy it is to make a classic hollandaise sauce with our simple method, the secrets of cooking asparagus spears – along with preparation tips, helpful hints and serving suggestions.

MAKING VINAIGRETTE DRESSING

A good vinaigrette can do more than dress a salad. It can also be used to baste meat, poultry, seafood or vegetables during cooking; and it can be used as a flavouring and tenderizing marinade. The basic mixture of oil, vinegar and seasoning lends itself to many variations.

The basic dressing will keep in the refrigerator, in a tightly closed container, for several weeks. Add flavourings, such as fresh herbs, just before using.

Makes just over 170ml/6fl oz
45ml/3 tbsp wine vinegar
salt and black pepper
150ml/¼ pint vegetable oil

1 Put the vinegar, salt and pepper in a bowl and whisk to dissolve the salt. Gradually add the oil, stirring with the whisk. Taste and adjust seasoning.

IDEAS FOR VINAIGRETTE

- Use a herb-flavoured vinegar.
- Use lemon juice instead of vinegar.
- Use olive oil, or a mixture of vegetable and olive oils.
- Use 120ml/4fl oz olive oil and 30ml/2 tbsp walnut or hazelnut oil.
- Add 15–30ml/1–2 tbsp Dijon mustard to the vinegar before whisking in the oil.
- Add 1 crushed garlic clove.
- Add 15–30ml/1–2 tbsp chopped fresh herbs (parsley, basil, chives, thyme, etc) to the vinaigrette.

MAKING MAYONNAISE

This cold emulsified sauce of oil and egg yolk has thousands of uses – as part of a dish or as an accompaniment, in sandwiches and in salad dressings. It can be varied by using different oils, vinegars and flavourings.

Makes about 360ml/12fl oz
2 egg yolks
360ml/12fl oz oil (vegetable, corn or olive)
15–30ml/1–2 tbsp lemon juice
5–10ml/1–2 tsp Dijon mustard
salt and black pepper

WATCHPOINT

Remember that foods containing raw eggs shouldn't be eaten by children, pregnant mothers, the elderly or the sick.

1 Beat the egg yolks in a bowl with a pinch of salt. Add the oil, 5–10ml/ 1–2 tsp at a time, beating constantly. After one-quarter of the oil has been added beat in 5–10ml/1–2 tsp of the lemon juice. Continue beating in the oil, in a thin, steady stream and as the mayonnaise thickens, add 5ml/1 tsp lemon juice.

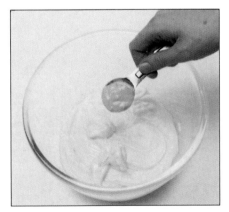

2 When all the oil has been beaten in, add the mustard. Taste the mayonnaise and add more lemon juice or vinegar. Season with salt and pepper. If the mayonnaise is too thick, beat in a spoonful or two of water. Home-made mayonnaise will keep, covered in the refrigerator, for up to 1 week. It should not be frozen.

MAKING SIMPLE HOLLANDAISE SAUCE

This classic of French cuisine has a reputation for being difficult to make. Harold McGee has devised a method of putting the ingredients in the pan at once, which lowers the chance of failure. Be careful not to allow the sauce to become too hot, or it will separate. Just take it slow and steady, and whisk constantly.

Makes about 300ml/½ pint/1¼ cups

3 egg yolks
15ml/1tbsp lemon juice, plus more
   if needed
a pinch of cayenne
salt and black pepper
225g/8oz/1 cup butter, preferable
   unsalted, cut into 15g/½oz/1 tbsp
   chunks

1 Combine the egg yolks, lemon juice, cayenne, salt and pepper in a heavy saucepan. Whisk together well. Add the butter and set the pan over moderate heat. Whisk constantly so that as the butter melts it is blended into the egg yolks.

2 When all the butter has melted and has been blended into the egg yolk base, continue whisking until the sauce just thickens to a creamy consistency. Taste the sauce and add more lemon juice, salt and pepper if needed.

PREPARING ASPARAGUS

When asparagus is young and tender, you need do nothing more than trim off the ends of the stalks. However, larger spears, with stalk ends that are tough and woody, require some further preparation.

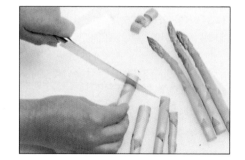

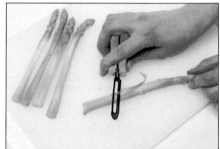

1 Cut off the tough, woody ends. Cut the spears so they are all about the same length.

2 If you like, remove the skin: lay a spear flat and hold it just below the tip. With a vegetable peeler, shave off the skin, working lengthways down the spear to the end of the stalk. Roll the spear so you can remove the skin from all sides.

ASPARAGUS WITH HOLLANDAISE SAUCE

Prepare 700g/1½lb asparagus. Arrange the spears on a rack in a steamer over simmering water, cover and steam for 8–12 minutes, or simmer in a large frying pan with water just to cover for 4–5 minutes, until just tender when pierced with the tip of a knife. Transfer to warmed plates and spoon over the Hollandaise sauce. *Serves 4.*

UPRIGHT COOKING

Asparagus spears can be cooked loose and flat in simmering water or tied into bundles and cooked standing upright in a tall pot. With the latter method, the tips are kept above the water so they cook gently in the steam.

PREPARING AND COOKING GLOBE ARTICHOKES

Artichokes can be served whole, with or without a stuffing, or just the meaty bottoms, or bases, may be used. Very small artichokes, 6cm/2½in or less in diameter, are often called hearts; this can be confusing, as artichoke bottoms are also sometimes called hearts. These baby artichokes are best braised whole, or halved or quartered. Be sure to rub all cut surfaces with lemon juice as you work and use a stainless steel knife, to prevent darkening and discoloration.

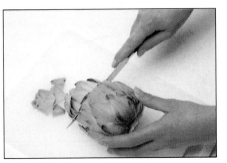

1 **Whole artichokes**: break off the stalk close to the base. Cut off the pointed top about one-third of the way down. Snip off the pointed end of each large outside leaf using scissors. Open up the leaves and rinse thoroughly between them.

2 **Artichoke bottoms**: break off all the coarse outer leaves down to the pale inner leaves. Scrape off the fuzzy centre, or 'choke' (or do this after cooking) and peel away all the leaves with a stainless steel knife, leaving just the edible base or bottom.

ARTICHOKES WITH HERB BUTTER

Serve boiled artichokes hot with clarified butter mixed with 15–30ml/1–2 tbsp chopped fresh dill and parsley or other herbs.

3 **To cook whole artichokes**: bring a large pot of salted water to the boil. Add the juice of 1 lemon or 45–60ml/3–4 tbsp vinegar. Add the prepared artichokes and put a plate on top to keep them submerged. Cover and simmer until you can pierce the stalk end easily with a fork: 15–20 minutes for small artichokes, 25–50 minutes for large artichokes.

4 Remove and drain well, upside-down. Open up the leaves so you can insert a spoon into the centre and scrape out the fuzzy choke.

EATING ARTICHOKES

One by one, pull off a leaf and dip the base into the sauce. Scrape the flesh from the base of the leaf with your teeth, then discard the leaf. When you have removed all the large leaves, you will have exposed the fuzzy choke. Scrape this off and discard it. Eat the meaty base with a fork.

5 **To cook artichoke bottoms**: boil gently in salted water to cover for 15–20 minutes or until tender.

IDEAS FOR ARTICHOKES

● Serve boiled artichokes hot with hollandaise sauce.
● Serve boiled artichokes cool (not chilled) with a vinaigrette dressing or mayonnaise.
● Serve cool artichoke bottoms filled with prawn or crab mayonnaise salad.
● Boil artichoke bottoms with flavourings such as garlic, bay leaf and black peppercorns. Drain and cool, then slice and marinate in a vinaigrette dressing with chopped onion and olives.

LIGHT SOUPS

A bowl of soup makes a tasty light meal or a flavourful starter, and before a substantial main course, soups that are neither too rich, nor too chunky are ideal. There are recipes here for everyday meals, and some deliciously different tastes to try when you are entertaining, such as Red Pepper Soup with Lime. Of course, the weather doesn't have to be cold for soup to be appealing, there are superb summer soups, too; choose from a creamy version of the classic Vichyssoise, a chilled avocado soup, or the spicy, yet refreshing Gazpacho.

Tomato and Basil Soup

In summer, when tomatoes are plentiful and cheap to buy, this is a lovely soup to make.

INGREDIENTS

Serves 4

30ml/2 tbsp olive oil
1 onion, chopped
2.5ml/½ tsp caster sugar
1 carrot, finely chopped
1 potato, finely chopped
1 garlic clove, crushed
675g/1½lb ripe tomatoes, roughly chopped
5ml/1 tsp tomato purée
1 bay leaf
1 thyme sprig
1 oregano sprig
4 basil leaves, roughly torn
300ml/½ pint/1¼ cups light chicken or vegetable stock
2–3 pieces sun-dried tomatoes in oil
30ml/2 tbsp shredded basil leaves
salt and black pepper

1 Heat the oil in a large pan, add the onion and sprinkle with the caster sugar. Cook gently for 5 minutes.

2 Add the chopped carrot and potato, cover the pan and cook over a low heat for a further 10 minutes, without browning the vegetables.

3 Stir in the garlic, tomatoes, tomato purée, herbs, stock and seasoning. Cover and cook gently for 25–30 minutes, until the vegetables are tender.

4 Remove the pan from the heat and press the soup through a sieve or food mill to extract all the skins and pips. Taste and adjust seasoning.

5 Reheat the soup gently, then ladle into four warmed soup bowls. Finely chop the sun-dried tomatoes and mix with a little oil from the jar. Add a spoonful to each serving, then scatter the shredded basil over the top.

Spiced Pumpkin Soup

INGREDIENTS

Serves 4

25g/1oz/2 tbsp butter
1 onion, finely chopped
1 small garlic clove, crushed
15ml/1 tbsp plain flour
pinch of grated nutmeg
2.5ml/½ tsp ground cinnamon
350g/12oz/3 cups pumpkin, seeded,
  peeled and cubed
600ml/1 pint/2½ cups chicken stock
150ml/¼ pint/²/₃ cup orange juice
5ml/1 tsp brown sugar
15ml/1 tbsp vegetable oil
2 slices Granary bread without crusts
30ml/2 tbsp sunflower seeds
salt and black pepper

1 Heat the butter in a large saucepan, add the onions and garlic and fry gently for 4–5 minutes, until softened.

2 Stir in the flour, spices and pumpkin, then cover and cook gently for 6 minutes, stirring occasionally.

3 Pour in the chicken stock and orange juice and add the brown sugar. Cover and bring to the boil, then reduce the heat and simmer for 20 minutes, until the pumpkin has softened.

4 Pour half of the mixture into a blender or food processor and whizz until smooth. Return the soup to the pan with the remaining chunky mixture, stirring constantly. Season well and heat through.

5 Meanwhile, make the croûtons. Heat the oil in a frying pan, cut the bread into cubes and fry gently until just beginning to brown. Add the sunflower seeds and fry for 1–2 minutes. Drain the croûtons on kitchen paper.

6 Serve the soup hot with a few of the croûtons scattered over the top. Serve the rest separately.

Chilled Leek and Potato Soup

This creamy, chilled soup is a version of the classic *Vichyssoise* originally created by a French chef at the Ritz Carlton Hotel in New York to celebrate the opening of the roof gardens.

INGREDIENTS

Serves 4

25g/1oz/2 tbsp butter
15ml/1 tbsp vegetable oil
1 small onion, chopped
3 leeks, sliced
2 potatoes, diced
600ml/1 pint/2½ cups vegetable stock
300ml/½ pint/1¼ cups milk
45ml/3 tbsp single cream
a little extra milk (optional)
salt and black pepper
60ml/4 tbsp natural yogurt and snipped chives, to garnish

1 Heat the butter and oil in a large saucepan and add the onion, leeks and potatoes. Cover and simmer for 15 minutes, stirring occasionally. Stir in the stock and milk and simmer for 10 minutes, until the potatoes are tender.

2 Ladle the vegetables and liquid into a blender or food processor in batches and purée until smooth. Return the soup to the pan, stir in the cream and season well.

3 Leave the soup to cool, and then chill for 3–4 hours, or until really cold. You may need to add a little extra milk to thin the soup down as it will thicken slightly as it cools.

4 Serve the chilled soup in individual bowls, topped with a spoonful of natural yogurt and a sprinkling of snipped fresh chives.

Curried Parsnip Soup

The spices impart a delicious, mild curry flavour which brings back memories of the Raj.

INGREDIENTS

Serves 4

25g/1oz/2 tbsp butter
1 garlic clove, crushed
1 onion, chopped
5ml/1 tsp ground cumin
5ml/1 tsp ground coriander
450g/1lb (about 4) parsnips, sliced
10ml/2 tsp medium curry paste
450ml/¾ pint/1⅞ cups chicken stock
450ml/¾ pint/1⅞ cups milk
60ml/4 tbsp soured cream
squeeze of lemon juice
salt and black pepper
fresh coriander sprigs, to garnish
ready-made garlic and coriander naan bread, to serve

1 Heat the butter in a large saucepan and add the garlic and onion. Fry gently for 4–5 minutes, until lightly golden. Stir in the spices and cook for a further 1–2 minutes.

2 Add the parsnips and stir until well coated with the butter, then stir in the curry paste, followed by the stock. Cover the pan and simmer for 15 minutes, until the parsnips are tender.

3 Ladle the soup into a blender or food processor and whizz until smooth. Return to the pan and stir in the milk. Heat gently for 2–3 minutes, then add 30ml/2 tbsp of the soured cream and the lemon juice. Season.

4 Serve in bowls topped with spoonfuls of the remaining soured cream and the fresh coriander accompanied by the naan bread.

Spiced Carrot Soup with Yogurt

Use a good home-made stock for this soup – it adds a far greater depth of flavour than stock made from cubes.

INGREDIENTS

Serves 4

50g/2oz/4 tbsp butter
3 leeks, sliced
450g/1lb carrots, sliced
15ml/1 tbsp ground coriander
1.2 litres/2 pints/5 cups chicken stock
150ml/¼ pint/⅔ cup Greek-style yogurt
30–45ml/2–3 tbsp chopped fresh coriander
salt and black pepper

1 Melt the butter in a large pan. Add the leeks and carrots and stir well, coating the vegetables with the butter. Cover and cook for about 10 minutes, until the vegetables are beginning to soften but not colour.

2 Stir in the ground coriander and cook for about 1 minute. Pour in the stock and add seasoning to taste. Bring to the boil, cover and simmer for about 20 minutes, until the leeks and carrots are tender.

3 Cool slightly, then purée the soup in a blender until smooth. Return to the pan and add 30ml/2 tbsp of the yogurt and the chopped fresh coriander. Taste and adjust the seasoning. Reheat gently but do not boil.

4 Ladle the soup into warmed soup bowls and put a spoonful of the remaining yogurt in the centre of each. Serve immediately.

Creamy Rocket Soup with Croûtons

Rocket, with its distinctive, peppery taste, is wonderful in this filling and satisfying soup. Serve it hot with ciabatta croûtons.

INGREDIENTS

Serves 4–6
50g/2oz/4 tbsp butter
1 onion, chopped
3 leeks, chopped
2 potatoes, diced
900ml/1½ pints/3¾ cups light chicken
    stock or water
2 large handfuls rocket, roughly
    chopped
150ml/¼ pint/⅔ cup double cream
salt and black pepper
garlic-flavoured ciabatta croûtons,
    to serve

1 Melt the butter in a large heavy-based pan, add the onion, leeks and potatoes and stir until the vegetables are coated in butter.

2 Cover and leave the vegetables to sweat for about 15 minutes. Pour in the stock, cover once again, then simmer for a further 20 minutes, until the vegetables are tender.

3 Press the soup through a sieve or food mill and return to the rinsed-out pan. (When puréeing the soup, don't use a blender or food processor, as these will give the soup a gluey texture.) Add the chopped rocket and cook gently for 5 minutes.

4 Stir in the cream, then season to taste and reheat gently. Ladle the soup into warmed soup bowls, then serve with a few garlic-flavoured ciabatta croûtons in each.

Rich Tomato Soup

A great British favourite – this fresh soup tastes so much nicer than the canned version. Make sure you use good-flavoured, ripe tomatoes, or home-grown.

INGREDIENTS

Serves 4

1kg/2lb (about 12 medium) tomatoes
15ml/1 tbsp olive oil
1 large onion, chopped
1 garlic clove, crushed
1 potato, chopped
15ml/1 tbsp tomato purée
5ml/1 tsp caster sugar
salt and black pepper
60ml/4 tbsp fromage frais
fresh chervil sprigs, to garnish

1 Place the tomatoes in a large heatproof bowl. Cover them with boiling water and leave to stand for about 1–2 minutes.

2 Heat the olive oil in a large pan and add the onion, garlic and potato. Fry gently for about 5 minutes, until the onion has softened.

3 Meanwhile, drain the hot water from the tomatoes, peel off the skins then halve the tomatoes and remove the cores. Chop the tomato flesh and add to the pan with the seeds, any juice and the tomato purée.

4 Pour over 300ml/½ pint/1¼ cups boiling water, stir, then cover and simmer gently for about 15 minutes, until the potato is soft.

5 Purée the soup in batches in a blender or food processor until smooth. Return the soup to the saucepan, add the sugar, season well and heat through. Serve in bowls with a dollop of fromage frais and the sprigs of fresh chervil.

French Onion Soup

INGREDIENTS

Serves 4

25g/1oz/2 tbsp butter
15ml/1 tbsp oil
3 large onions, thinly sliced
5ml/1 tsp soft brown sugar
15ml/1 tbsp plain flour
2 x 300g/10oz cans condensed beef consommé
30ml/2 tbsp medium sherry
10ml/2 tsp Worcestershire sauce
8 slices French bread
15ml/1 tbsp French coarse-grained mustard
75g/3oz/1 cup Gruyère cheese, grated
salt and black pepper
15ml/1 tbsp chopped fresh parsley, to garnish

1 Heat the butter and oil in a large saucepan and add the onions and brown sugar. Cook gently for about 20 minutes, stirring occasionally, until the onions start to turn golden brown.

2 Stir in the flour and cook for a further 2 minutes. Pour in the consommé, plus two cans of water, then add the sherry and Worcestershire sauce. Season well, cover and simmer gently for a further 25–30 minutes.

3 Preheat the grill and just before serving, toast the bread lightly on both sides. Spread one side of each slice with the mustard and top with the grated cheese. Grill the toasts until bubbling and golden.

4 Ladle the soup into bowls. Pop two croûtons on top of each bowl of soup and garnish with chopped fresh parsley. Serve at once.

Watercress and Orange Soup

This is a very healthy and refreshing soup, which is just as good served hot or chilled.

Ingredients

Serves 4

1 large onion, chopped
15ml/1 tbsp olive oil
2 bunches or bags of watercress
grated rind and juice of l large orange
1 vegetable stock cube
150ml/¼ pint/⅔ cup single cream
10ml/2 tsp cornflour
salt and black pepper
a little thick cream or yogurt,
  to garnish
4 orange wedges, to serve

1 Soften the onion in the oil in a large pan. Trim any big stalks off the watercress, then add to the pan of onion without chopping. Cover the pan and cook the watercress for about 5 minutes until softened.

2 Add the orange rind and juice, and the stock cube dissolved in 600ml/ 1 pint/2½ cups water. Bring to the boil, cover and simmer for 10–15 minutes.

3 Blend or liquidize the soup thoroughly, and sieve if you like. Add the cream blended with the cornflour, and seasoning to taste.

4 Bring the soup gently back to the boil, stirring until just slightly thickened. Check the seasoning and serve the soup with a swirl of cream or yogurt, and a wedge of orange to squeeze in at the last moment.

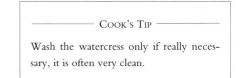

—————— Cook's Tip ——————

Wash the watercress only if really necessary, it is often very clean.

Mushroom and Herb Soup

Although you can make mushroom soup with a nice smooth texture, it is more time consuming and you waste a lot of mushrooms – so enjoy the slightly nutty consistency instead!

INGREDIENTS

Serves 4

50g/2oz smoked streaky bacon
1 white onion, chopped
15ml/1 tbsp sunflower oil
350g/12oz flat cap field mushrooms or a mixture of wild and brown mushrooms
600ml/1 pint/2½ cups good meat stock
30ml/2 tbsp sweet sherry
30ml/2 tbsp chopped, mixed fresh herbs, such as sage, rosemary, thyme or marjoram, or 10ml/2 tsp dried
salt and black pepper
60ml/4 tbsp thick Greek-style yogurt or crème fraîche and a few sprigs of marjoram or sage, to garnish

1 Roughly chop the bacon and place in a large saucepan. Cook gently until all the fat comes out of the bacon.

2 Add the onion and soften, adding oil if necessary. Wipe the mushrooms clean, roughly chop and add to the pan. Cover and sweat until they have completely softened and their liquid has run out.

3 Add the stock, sherry, herbs and seasoning, cover and simmer for 10-12 minutes. Blend or liquidize the soup until smooth, but don't worry if you still have a slightly textured result.

4 Check the seasoning and heat through. Serve with a dollop of yogurt or crème fraîche and a herb sprig in each bowl.

Carrot and Coriander Soup

Carrot soup is best made with young carrots when they are at their sweetest and tastiest. With older carrots you will have to use more to get the full flavour. This soup freezes well.

INGREDIENTS

Serves 5–6

1 onion, chopped
15ml/1 tbsp sunflower oil
675g/1½lb carrots, chopped
900ml/1½ pint/3¾ cups chicken stock
few sprigs fresh coriander, or 5ml/1 tsp dried
5ml/1 tsp lemon rind
30ml/2 tbsp lemon juice
salt and black pepper
chopped fresh parsley or coriander, to garnish

1 Soften the onion in the oil in a large pan. Add the chopped carrots, the stock, coriander leaves, lemon rind and juice and seasoning to taste.

2 Bring to the boil, cover and simmer for 15–20 minutes, occasionally checking that there is sufficient liquid. When the carrots are really tender, blend or liquidize and return to the pan, then check the seasoning.

3 Heat through again and sprinkle with chopped parsley or coriander before serving.

Prawn and Sweetcorn Chowder

This soup is perfect for informal entertaining as it is quite special but not too extravagant.

INGREDIENTS

Serves 4

15g/½oz/1 tbsp butter
1 onion, chopped
300g/11oz can sweetcorn
30ml/2 tbsp lemon juice
300ml/½ pint/1¼ cups fish or vegetable stock
115g/4oz/1 cup cooked, peeled prawns
300ml/½ pint/1¼ cups milk
15–30ml/1–2 tbsp cream or yogurt
salt and black pepper
4 large prawns in their shells and a few sprigs parsley or dill, to garnish

1 Heat the butter in a pan and cook the onions until translucent. Add half the sweetcorn and all its liquid, the lemon juice, stock and half the prawns.

2 Cover and simmer the soup for about 15 minutes, then blend or liquidize the soup until quite smooth.

3 Return the soup to the pan and add the milk, the rest of the prawns, chopped, and the sweetcorn, the cream or yogurt and seasoning to taste. Cook gently for 5 minutes, or until reduced sufficiently.

4 Serve each portion garnished with a whole prawn and a herb sprig.

Chilled Avocado Soup

INGREDIENTS

Serves 4

2 large or 3 medium ripe avocados
15ml/1 tbsp fresh lemon juice
¼ cucumber, peeled and coarsely
    chopped
30ml/2 tbsp dry sherry
4 spring onions, roughly chopped
475ml/16fl oz/2 cups chicken stock
a few drops of Tabasco sauce (optional)
salt
natural yogurt or soured cream,
    to serve

1 Halve the avocados, remove the stones, and peel. Roughly chop the flesh and place in a food processor or blender. Add the lemon juice and process until very smooth.

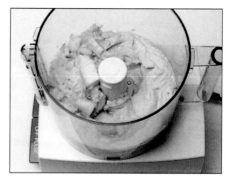

2 Add the cucumber, sherry and most of the chopped spring onions. Process again until very smooth.

3 Transfer the avocado mixture to a large bowl, add the chicken stock and whisk until well blended. Season the soup with salt to taste and Tabasco sauce, if desired. Cover the bowl with clear film and chill well.

4 To serve, pour the soup into individual bowls. Swirl a spoonful of yogurt or soured cream in the centre of each bowl. Sprinkle with the reserved spring onions.

Green Pea and Mint Soup

This soup is equally delicious cold. Instead of reheating it after purée-ing, leave it to cool and then chill lightly in the fridge. Stir in the swirl of cream just before serving.

INGREDIENTS

Serves 4
50g/2oz/4 tbsp butter
4 spring onions, chopped
450g/1lb fresh or frozen peas
600ml/1 pint/2½ cups chicken or vegetable stock
2 large mint sprigs
600 ml/1 pint/2½ cups milk
pinch of sugar (optional)
salt and pepper
single cream, to serve
small mint sprigs, to garnish

1 Heat the butter in a large saucepan, add the spring onions, and cook gently for a few minutes until softened but not coloured.

FREEZER NOTE

The soup can be frozen for up to two months after step 2. Allow it to thaw in the fridge before puréeing and reheating.

---

2 Stir the peas into the pan, add the stock and mint and bring to the boil. Cover and simmer very gently for about 30 minutes for fresh peas or 15 minutes if you are using frozen peas, until the peas are very tender. Remove about 45ml/3 tbsp of the peas using a slotted spoon, and reserve for the garnish.

3 Pour the soup into a food processor or blender, add the milk and purée until smooth. Then return the soup to the pan and reheat gently. Season to taste, adding a pinch of sugar, if liked.

4 Pour the soup into bowls. Swirl a little cream into each, then garnish with mint and the reserved peas.

Beetroot and Apricot Swirl

This soup is most attractive if you swirl together the two coloured mixtures, but if you prefer they can be mixed together to save on time and dishes.

INGREDIENTS 🍎

Serves 4

4 large cooked beetroots, coarsely
   chopped
1 small onion, coarsely chopped
600ml/1 pint/2½ cups chicken stock
200g/7oz/1 cup dried apricots
250ml/8fl oz/1 cup orange juice
salt and black pepper

1 Place the beetroots and half the onion in a pan with the stock. Bring to the boil, then reduce the heat, cover, and simmer for about 10 minutes. Purée in a food processor or blender.

2 Place the rest of the onion in a pan with the apricots and orange juice, cover, and simmer gently for about 15 minutes, until tender. Purée in a food processor or blender.

3 Return the two mixtures to the saucepans and reheat. Season to taste with salt and pepper, then swirl them together in individual soup bowls for a marbled effect.

COOK'S TIP

The apricot mixture should be the same consistency as the beetroot mixture – if it is too thick, then add a little more orange juice to thin it slightly.

Red Pepper Soup with Lime

The beautiful rich red colour of this soup makes it a very attractive starter or light lunch. For a special dinner, toast some tiny croûtons and serve sprinkled into the soup.

INGREDIENTS 🍎

Serves 4–6
4 red peppers, seeded and chopped
1 large onion, chopped
5ml/1 tsp olive oil
1 garlic clove, crushed
1 small red chilli, sliced
45ml/3 tbsp tomato pureé
900ml/1½ pints/3¾ cups chicken stock
finely grated rind and juice of 1 lime
salt and black pepper
shreds of lime rind, to garnish

1 Cook the onion and peppers gently in the oil in a covered saucepan for about 5 minutes, shaking the pan occasionally, until softened.

2 Stir in the garlic, then add the chilli with the tomato purée. Stir in half the stock, then bring to the boil. Cover the pan and simmer for 10 minutes.

3 Cool slightly, then purée in a food processor or blender. Return to the pan, then add the remaining stock, the lime rind and juice, and seasoning.

4 Bring the soup back to the boil, then serve at once with strips of lime rind scattered into each bowl.

COOK'S TIP

Yellow or orange peppers could be substituted for the red peppers. And, if you don't have a fresh chilli, add a dash or two of Tabasco sauce to the soup instead.

Pasta and Tomato Soup

Children will love this soup – especially if you use fancy pieces of pasta such as alphabet or animal shapes.

INGREDIENTS 🍎

Serves 4
675g/1½lb ripe plum tomatoes
1 medium onion, quartered
1 celery stick
1 garlic clove
15ml/1 tbsp olive oil
450ml/¾ pint/1⅞ cups chicken stock
30ml/2 tbsp tomato purée
50g/2oz/½ cup small pasta shapes
salt and black pepper
fresh coriander or parsley, to garnish

1 Place the tomatoes, onion, celery, and garlic in a pan with the oil. Cover and cook over low heat for 40–45 minutes, shaking the pan occasionally, until very soft.

2 Spoon the vegetables into a food processor or blender and process until smooth. Press through a sieve, then return to the pan.

3 Stir in the stock and tomato purée and bring to the boil. Add the pasta and simmer gently for about 8 minutes, or until the pasta is tender. Add salt and pepper to taste, then sprinkle with coriander or parsley and serve hot.

— COOK'S TIP —

If fresh plum tomatoes are not available, then use other flavourful, red, ripe tomatoes, or substitute canned tomatoes.

Mushroom, Celery and Garlic Soup

INGREDIENTS 🍎

Serves 4
350g/12oz/3 cups chopped mushrooms
4 celery sticks, chopped
3 garlic cloves
45ml/3 tbsp dry sherry or white wine
750ml/1¼ pints/3⅔ cups chicken stock
30ml/2 tbsp Worcestershire sauce
5ml/1 tsp ground nutmeg
salt and black pepper
celery leaves, to garnish

1 Place the mushrooms, celery, and garlic in a pan and stir in the sherry or wine. Cover and cook over low heat for 30–40 minutes, until tender.

2 Add half the stock and purée in a food processor or blender until smooth. Return to the pan and add the remaining stock, the Worcestershire sauce, and nutmeg.

3 Bring to the boil, season, and serve hot, garnished with celery leaves.

— COOK'S TIP —

To make this flavoursome soup suitable for vegetarians, use vegetable stock in place of the chicken stock.

Cauliflower and Walnut Cream

Even though there's no cream added to this soup, the cauliflower gives it a delicious, rich, creamy texture.

INGREDIENTS

Serves 4
1 medium cauliflower
1 medium onion, coarsely chopped
450ml/¾ pint/1⅞ cups chicken or
    vegetable stock
450ml/¾ pint/1⅞ cups skimmed milk
45ml/3 tbsp walnut pieces
salt and black pepper
paprika and chopped walnuts,
    to garnish

1 Trim the cauliflower of outer leaves and break into small florets. Place the cauliflower, onion, and stock in a large saucepan.

2 Bring to the boil, cover, and simmer for about 15 minutes, or until soft. Add the milk and walnuts, then purée in a food processor until smooth.

3 Season the soup to taste, then bring to the boil. Serve sprinkled with paprika and chopped walnuts.

VARIATIONS

To make Cauliflower and Almond Cream, use 45ml/3 tbsp ground almonds in place of the walnut pieces.

Curried Carrot and Apple Soup

INGREDIENTS

Serves 4
10ml/2 tsp sunflower oil
15ml/1 tbsp mild curry powder
500g/1¼lb carrots, chopped
1 large onion, chopped
1 cooking apple, chopped
750ml/1¼ pints/3⅔ cups chicken stock
salt and black pepper
plain low fat yogurt and carrot curls,
    to garnish

COOK'S TIP

Choose an acidic apple that will soften and fluff up as it cooks. Chop it into fairly small pieces before adding to the pan.

---

1 Heat the oil and gently fry the curry powder for 2–3 minutes.

2 Add the carrots, onion, and apple, stir well, then cover the pan.

3 Cook over very low heat for about 15 minutes, shaking the pan occasionally until softened. Spoon the vegetable mixture into a food processor or blender, then add half the stock and process until smooth.

4 Return to the pan and pour in the remaining stock. Bring the soup to the boil and adjust the seasoning before serving in bowls, garnished with a swirl of yogurt and a few curls of carrot.

Gazpacho

INGREDIENTS

Serves 4

½ cucumber (about 225g/8oz),
 coarsely chopped
½ green pepper, seeded and coarsely
 chopped
½ red pepper, seeded and coarsely
 chopped
1 large tomato, coarsely chopped
2 spring onions, chopped
Tabasco sauce (optional)
45ml/3 tbsp chopped fresh parsley or
 coriander, to garnish
croûtons, to serve

For the soup base

450g/1lb ripe tomatoes, peeled, seeded
 and chopped
15ml/1 tbsp tomato ketchup
30ml/2 tbsp tomato purée
1.25ml/¼ tsp sugar
3.75ml/¾ tsp salt
5ml/1 tsp black pepper
45ml/3 tbsp sherry vinegar
175ml/6fl oz/¾ cup olive oil
350ml/12fl oz/1½ cups tomato juice

1 First make the soup base. Put the
tomatoes in a food processor or
blender and pulse on and off until just
smooth, scraping the sides of the container occasionally.

— COOK'S TIP —

Use extra virgin olive oil in this soup for the
very best flavour.

2 Add the ketchup, tomato purée,
sugar, salt, pepper, vinegar and oil
and pulse on and off three or four
times, just to blend. Transfer to a large
bowl and stir in the tomato juice.

3 Place the cucumber and green and
red peppers in the food processor
or blender and pulse on and off until
finely chopped; do not overmix.

4 Reserve about 30ml/2 tbsp of the
chopped vegetables for garnishing;
stir the remainder into the soup. Taste
for seasoning. Mix in the chopped
tomato, spring onions and a dash of
Tabasco sauce, if desired. Chill well.

5 To serve, ladle into bowls and
sprinkle with the reserved chopped
vegetables, chopped fresh parsley or
coriander and the croûtons.

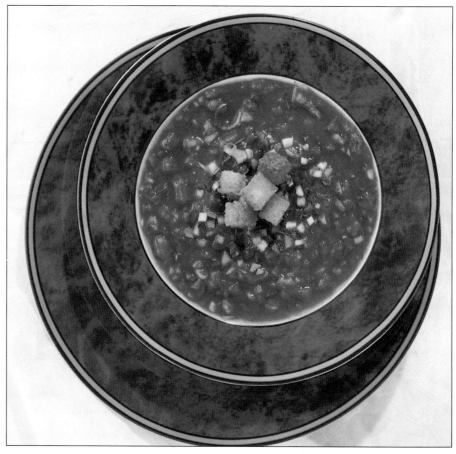

Thai-style Corn Soup

This is a very quick and easy soup, made in minutes. If you are using frozen prawns, then defrost them first before adding to the soup.

INGREDIENTS

Serves 4

2.5ml/½ tsp sesame or sunflower oil
2 spring onions, thinly sliced
1 garlic clove, crushed
600ml/1 pint/2½ cups chicken stock
425g/15oz can creamed corn
225g/8oz/1¼ cups cooked, peeled
  prawns
5ml/1 tsp green chilli paste or chilli
  sauce (optional)
salt and black pepper
fresh coriander leaves, to garnish

1 Heat the oil in a large heavy-based saucepan and sauté the spring onions and garlic over medium heat for about 1 minute, until softened, but not browned.

2 Stir in the chicken stock, creamed corn, prawns, and chilli paste or sauce, if using.

3 Bring the soup to the boil, stirring occasionally. Season to taste, then serve at once, sprinkled with fresh coriander leaves to garnish.

COOK'S TIP

If creamed corn is not available, use ordinary canned sweetcorn, puréed in a food processor for a few seconds, until creamy yet with some texture left.

VARIATIONS

To make Thai-style Crab and Corn Soup, use canned or freshly cooked crab in place of all or some of the prawns.

SUBSTANTIAL SOUPS

Soups are richly warming, perfect for the starving hordes on a winter's day, and, served with crusty bread, pesto-topped toasts, or crunchy croûtons, they make a filling lunch or supper. Some of the tastiest and best soups are traditional recipes: try Cock-a-leekie, or Scotch Broth from Scotland, Italian Minestrone, or thick and delicious Split Pea and Bacon Soup. Or, for a special occasion, fish or shellfish soups are also excellent as a meal – choose Mussel Bisque for an informal supper with friends, or try a tasty bowl of Corn and Crab Chowder.

Jerusalem Artichoke Soup

Topped with saffron cream, this
soup is wonderful on a chilly day.

INGREDIENTS

Serves 4
50g/2oz/4 tbsp butter
1 onion, chopped
450g/1lb Jerusalem artichokes, peeled
  and cut into chunks
900ml/1½ pints/3¾ cups chicken stock
150ml/¼ pint/⅔ cup milk
150ml/¼ pint/⅔ cup double cream
good pinch of saffron powder
salt and black pepper
snipped fresh chives, to garnish

1 Melt the butter in a large heavy-
based pan and cook the onion for
5–8 minutes, until soft but not
browned, stirring occasionally.

2 Add the artichokes to the pan and
stir until coated in the butter. Cover
and cook gently for 10–15 minutes;
do not allow the artichokes to brown.
Pour in the stock and milk, then cover
and simmer for 15 minutes. Cool
slightly, then process in a blender or
food processor until smooth.

3 Strain the soup back into the pan.
Add half the cream, season to taste,
and reheat gently. Lightly whip the
remaining cream and saffron powder.
Ladle the soup into warmed soup bowls
and put a spoonful of saffron cream
in the centre of each. Scatter over the
snipped chives and serve at once.

Broccoli and Stilton Soup

A really easy, but rich, soup –
choose something simple to
follow, such as plainly roasted
or grilled meat, poultry or fish.

INGREDIENTS

Serves 4
350g/12oz broccoli
25g/1oz/2 tbsp butter
1 onion, chopped
1 leek, white part only, chopped
1 small potato, cut into chunks
600ml/1 pint/2½ cups hot
  chicken stock
300ml/½ pint/1¼ cups milk
45ml/3 tbsp double cream
115g/4oz Stilton cheese, rind removed,
  crumbled
salt and black pepper

1 Break the broccoli into florets,
discarding tough stems. Set aside
two small florets for the garnish.

2 Melt the butter in a large pan and
cook the onion and leek until soft
but not coloured. Add the broccoli and
potato, then pour in the stock. Cover
and simmer for 15–20 minutes, until
the vegetables are tender.

3 Cool slightly, then purée in a
blender or food processor. Strain
through a sieve back into the pan.

4 Add the milk, cream and seasoning
to the pan and reheat gently. At the
last minute add the cheese, stirring until
it just melts. Do not boil.

5 Meanwhile, blanch the reserved
broccoli florets and cut them
vertically into thin slices. Ladle the
soup into warmed bowls and garnish
with the broccoli florets and a generous
grinding of black pepper.

Salmon Chowder

INGREDIENTS

Serves 4

25g/1oz/2 tbsp butter or margarine
1 onion, finely chopped
1 leek, finely chopped
1 fennel bulb, finely chopped
30ml/2 tbsp plain flour
1.2 litres/2 pints/5 cups fish stock
2 medium-size potatoes, cut into
  1cm/½in cubes
450g/1lb boneless, skinless salmon, cut
  into 2cm/¾in cubes
175ml/6fl oz/¾ cup milk
120ml/4fl oz/½ cup single cream
30ml/2 tbsp chopped fresh dill
salt and black pepper

1 Melt the butter or margarine in a large saucepan. Add the onion, leek and fennel and cook over a medium heat for 5–8 minutes, until softened, stirring occasionally.

2 Stir in the flour. Reduce the heat to low and cook, stirring occasionally, for a further 3 minutes.

3 Add the stock and potatoes and season with salt and pepper. Bring to the boil, then reduce the heat, cover, and simmer for about 20 minutes, until the potatoes are tender.

4 Add the salmon cubes and simmer for 3–5 minutes, until just cooked.

5 Stir in the milk, cream and dill and cook until just warmed through; do not boil. Taste and adjust the seasoning, if necessary, then serve.

Leek and Potato Soup

The chopped vegetables in this recipe produce a really chunky soup. If you prefer a smooth texture, press the mixture through a sieve or purée it in a food mill.

INGREDIENTS

Serves 4

50g/2oz/4 tbsp butter
2 leeks, chopped
1 small onion, finely chopped
350g/12oz potatoes, chopped
900ml/1½ pints/3¾ cups chicken or
    vegetable stock
salt and pepper

1 Heat 25g/1oz/2 tbsp of the butter in a large saucepan, add the leeks and onions and cook gently, stirring occasionally, for about 7 minutes, until softened but not browned.

COOK'S TIP

Don't use a food processor to purée this soup as it can make the potatoes gluey.

2 Add the potatoes to the pan and cook, stirring occasionally, for 2–3 minutes, then add the stock and bring to the boil. Cover the pan and simmer gently for 30–35 minutes, until the vegetables are very tender.

3 Adjust the seasoning, remove the pan from the heat and stir in the remaining butter in small pieces. Serve hot with crusty bread.

Chicken Broth with Cheese Toasts

INGREDIENTS

Serves 4

1 roasted chicken carcass
1 onion, quartered
2 celery sticks, finely chopped
1 garlic clove, crushed
few sprigs parsley
2 bay leaves
225g/8oz can chopped tomatoes
200g/7oz can chick-peas
30–45ml/2–3 tbsp leftover vegetables,
   chopped, or 1 large carrot, finely
   chopped
15ml/1 tbsp chopped fresh parsley
2 slices toast
25g/1oz/¼ cup grated cheese
salt and black pepper

1 Pick off any little bits of flesh from the carcass, especially from the underside where there is often some very tasty dark meat. Put aside.

2 Place the carcass, broken in half, in a large pan with the onion, half the celery, the garlic, herbs and sufficient water to cover. Cover the pan, bring to the boil and simmer for about 30 minutes, or until you are left with about 300ml/½ pint/1¼ cups of liquid.

3 Strain the stock and return to the pan. Add the chicken flesh, the remaining celery, the tomatoes, chick-peas (and their liquid), vegetables and parsley. Season to taste and simmer for another 7–10 minutes.

4 Meanwhile, sprinkle the toast with the cheese and grill until bubbling. Cut the toast into fingers or quarters and serve with, or floating on top of, the finished soup.

Bread and Cheese Soup

INGREDIENTS

Serves 4

115g/4oz strong-flavoured or blue
   cheese, or 175g/6oz mild cheese
600ml/1 pint/2½ cups semi-skimmed
   milk
few pinches ground mace
4–6 slices stale bread
30ml/2 tbsp olive oil
1 large garlic clove, crushed
salt and black pepper
15ml/1 tbsp snipped chives, to garnish

1 Remove any rinds from the cheese and grate into a heavy-based, preferably non-stick pan. Add the milk and heat through very slowly, stirring frequently to make sure it does not stick and burn.

2 When all the cheese has melted, add the mace, seasoning, and one piece of crustless bread. Cook over a very gentle heat until the bread has softened and slightly thickened the soup.

3 Mix the oil with the garlic and brush over the remaining bread. Toast until crisp, then cut into triangles or fingers. Sprinkle the soup with chives and serve with the toast.

COOK'S TIP

Don't mix blue cheeses with other kinds of cheese in this soup.

Split Pea and Courgette Soup

Rich and satisfying, this tasty and nutritious soup will warm you on a chilly winter's day.

INGREDIENTS 🍎

Serves 4

175g/6oz/1⅞ cups yellow
   split peas
1 medium onion, finely chopped
5ml/1 tsp sunflower oil
2 medium courgettes, finely diced
900ml/1½ pints/3¾ cups chicken
   stock
2.5ml/½ tsp ground turmeric
salt and black pepper

1 Place the split peas in a bowl, cover with cold water, and leave to soak for several hours or overnight. Drain, rinse in cold water, and drain again.

2 Cook the onion in the oil in a covered pan, shaking occasionally, until soft. Reserve a handful of diced courgettes and add the rest to the pan. Cook, stirring, for 2–3 minutes.

3 Add the stock and turmeric to the pan and bring to the boil. Reduce the heat, then cover and simmer for 30–40 minutes, or until the split peas are tender. Adjust the seasoning.

4 When the soup is almost ready, bring a large saucepan of water to the boil, add the reserved diced courgettes, and cook for 1 minute, then drain and add to the soup before serving hot with warm crusty bread.

COOK'S TIP

For a quicker alternative, use split red lentils for this soup – they need no pre-soaking and cook very quickly. Adjust the amount of stock, if necessary.

VARIATION

To add a little extra colour and flavour, stir in some peeled and seeded strips of fresh ripe red tomatoes.

Pasta and Bean Soup

Serve this hearty main-meal soup with tasty, pesto-topped French bread croûtons.

INGREDIENTS

Serves 4

115g/4oz/²⁄₃ cup dry beans (a mixture
 of red kidney and haricot beans),
 soaked in cold water overnight
15ml/1 tbsp oil
1 onion, chopped
2 celery sticks, thinly sliced
2–3 garlic cloves, crushed
2 leeks, thinly sliced
1 vegetable stock cube
400g/14oz can or jar of pimientos
45–60ml/3–4 tbsp tomato purée
115g/4oz pasta shapes
4 pieces French bread
15ml/1 tbsp pesto sauce
115g/4oz/1 cup baby sweetcorn,
 halved
50g/2oz each broccoli and cauliflower
 florets
few drops of Tabasco sauce, to taste
salt and black pepper

1 Drain the beans and place in a large pan with 1.2 litres/2 pints/5 cups water. Bring to the boil and simmer for about 1 hour, or until nearly tender.

2 When the beans are almost ready, heat the oil in a large pan and fry the vegetables for 2 minutes. Add the stock cube and the beans with about 600ml/1 pint/2 cups of their liquid. Cover and simmer for 10 minutes.

3 Meanwhile, purée the pimientos with a little of their liquid and add to the pan. Stir in the tomato purée and pasta and cook for 15 minutes. Preheat the oven to 200°C/400°F/Gas 6.

4 Meanwhile, make the pesto croûtons; spread the French bread with the pesto sauce and bake for 10 minutes, or until crispy.

5 When the pasta is just cooked, add the sweetcorn, broccoli and cauliflower florets, Tabasco sauce and seasoning to taste. Heat through for 2–3 minutes and serve at once with the pesto croûtons.

Country Vegetable Soup

To ring the changes, vary the vegetables according to what is in season – or in the market.

INGREDIENTS

Serves 4
50g/2oz/4 tbsp butter
1 onion, chopped
2 leeks, sliced
2 celery sticks, sliced
2 carrots, sliced
2 small turnips, chopped
4 ripe tomatoes, skinned and chopped
1 litre/1¾ pints/4 cups chicken, veal or
    vegetable stock
bouquet garni
115g/4oz green beans, chopped
salt and pepper
chopped herbs such as tarragon, thyme,
    chives and parsley, to garnish

1 Heat the butter in a large saucepan, add the onion and leeks and cook gently until soft but not coloured.

2 Add the celery, carrots and turnips and cook for 3–4 minutes, stirring occasionally. Stir in the tomatoes and stock, add the bouquet garni and simmer for about 20 minutes.

3 Add the beans to the soup and cook until all the vegetables are tender. Season to taste and serve garnished with chopped herbs.

Split Pea and Bacon Soup

Another name for this tasty old-fashioned soup is 'London Particular', from the dense fogs for which the city used to be notorious. The fogs in turn were named 'pea-soupers'.

INGREDIENTS

Serves 4
15g/½oz/1 tbsp butter
115g/4oz smoked back bacon,
    chopped
1 large onion, chopped
1 carrot, chopped
1 celery stick, chopped
75g/3oz/scant ½ cup split peas
1.2 litres/2 pints/5 cups chicken stock
salt and pepper
2 thick slices firm bread, buttered and
    without crusts
2 streaky bacon rashers

1 Heat the butter in a saucepan, add the back bacon and cook until the fat runs. Stir in the onion, carrot and celery and cook for 2–3 minutes.

2 Add the split peas followed by the stock. Bring to the boil, stirring occasionally, then cover and simmer for 45–60 minutes.

3 Meanwhile, preheat the oven to 180°C/350°F/Gas 4 and bake the bread for about 20 minutes, until crisp and brown, then cut into cubes.

4 Grill the streaky bacon until very crisp, then chop finely.

5 When the soup is ready to be served, season to taste and garnish with chopped bacon and croutons scattered on each portion.

Minestrone with Pesto Toasts

This Italian mixed vegetable soup comes originally from Genoa, but the vegetables vary from region to region. This is also a great way to use up leftover vegetables.

INGREDIENTS

Serves 4
30ml/2 tbsp olive oil
2 garlic cloves, crushed
1 onion, halved and sliced
225g/8oz/2 cups diced lean bacon
2 small courgettes, quartered
  and sliced
50g/2oz/½ cup French beans, chopped
2 small carrots, diced
2 celery sticks, finely chopped
bouquet garni
50g/2oz/½ cup short cut macaroni
50g/2oz/½ cup frozen peas
200g/7oz can red kidney beans,
  drained and rinsed
50g/2oz/1 cup shredded green cabbage
4 tomatoes, skinned and seeded
salt and black pepper

For the toasts
8 slices French bread
15ml/1 tbsp ready-made pesto sauce
15ml/1 tbsp grated Parmesan cheese

1 Heat the oil in a large pan and gently fry the garlic and onions for 5 minutes, until just softened. Add the bacon, courgettes, French beans, carrots and celery to the pan and stir-fry for a further 3 minutes.

2 Pour 1.1 litres/2 pints/5 cups of cold water over the vegetables and add the bouquet garni. Cover the pan and simmer for 25 minutes.

3 Add the macaroni, peas and kidney beans and cook for 8 minutes. Then add the cabbage and tomatoes and cook for a further 5 minutes.

4 Meanwhile, spread the bread slices with the pesto, sprinkle a little Parmesan over each one and brown lightly under a hot grill.

5 Remove the bouquet garni, season the soup and serve with the toasts.

--- COOK'S TIP ---

If you like, to appeal to children, you could replace the macaroni with coloured pasta shapes such as shells, twists or bows.

Mulligatawny

Mulligatawny (which means 'pepper water') was introduced into England in the late eighteenth century by members of the army and colonial service returning home from India.

INGREDIENTS

Serves 4

50g/2oz/4 tbsp butter or 60ml/
   4 tbsp oil
2 large chicken joints, about 350g/
   12oz each
1 onion, chopped
1 carrot, chopped
1 small turnip, chopped
about 15ml/1 tbsp curry powder,
   to taste
4 cloves
6 black peppercorns, lightly crushed
50g/2oz/¼ cup lentils
900ml/1½ pints/3¾ cups chicken stock
40g/1½oz/¼ cup sultanas
salt and black pepper

2 Add the onion, carrot and turnip to the pan and cook, stirring occasionally, until lightly coloured. Stir in the curry powder, cloves and peppercorns and cook for 1–2 minutes, then add the lentils.

3 Pour the stock into the pan, bring to the boil, then add the sultanas and chicken and any juices from the plate. Cover the pan and simmer gently for about 1¼ hours.

4 Remove the chicken from the pan and discard the skin and bones. Chop the flesh, return to the soup and reheat. Check the seasoning before serving the soup piping hot.

1 Melt the butter or heat the oil in a large saucepan, then brown the chicken over a brisk heat. Transfer the chicken to a plate.

COOK'S TIP

Choose red split lentils for the best colour, although either green or brown lentils could also be used.

Cock-a-Leekie

This traditional soup recipe – it is known from as long ago as 1598 – originally included beef as well as chicken. In the past it would have been made from an old cock bird, hence the name.

INGREDIENTS

Serves 4–6
2 chicken portions, about 275g/
   10oz each
1.2 litres/2 pints/5 cups chicken stock
bouquet garni
4 leeks
8–12 prunes, soaked
salt and black pepper
soft buttered rolls, to serve

1 Gently cook the chicken, stock and bouquet garni for 40 minutes.

2 Cut the white part of the leeks into 2.5cm/1in slices and thinly slice a little of the green part.

3 Add the white part of the leeks and the prunes to the saucepan and cook gently for 20 minutes, then add the green part of the leeks and cook for a further 10–15 minutes.

4 Discard the bouquet garni. Remove the chicken from the pan, discard the skin and bones and chop the flesh. Return the chicken to the pan and season the soup. Heat the soup through, then serve hot with soft buttered rolls.

Scotch Broth

Sustaining and warming, Scotch Broth is custom-made for chilly Scottish weather, and makes a delicious winter soup anywhere.

INGREDIENTS

Serves 6–8
1kg/2lb lean neck of lamb, cut into
   large, even-sized chunks
1.75 litres/3 pints/7½ cups water
1 large onion, chopped
50g/2oz/¼ cup pearl barley
bouquet garni
1 large carrot, chopped
1 turnip, chopped
3 leeks, chopped
½ small white cabbage, shredded
salt and black pepper
chopped parsley, to serve

1 Put the lamb and water into a large saucepan and bring to the boil. Skim off the scum, then stir in the onion, barley and bouquet garni.

2 Bring the soup back to the boil, then partly cover the saucepan and simmer gently for 1 hour. Add the remaining vegetables and the seasoning to the pan. Bring to the boil, partly cover again and simmer for about 35 minutes until the vegetables are tender.

3 Remove surplus fat from the top of the soup, then serve hot, sprinkled with chopped parsley.

Thai Chicken Soup

INGREDIENTS

Serves 4

15ml/1 tbsp vegetable oil
1 garlic clove, finely chopped
2 x 175g/6oz boned chicken breasts, skinned and chopped
2.5ml/½ tsp ground turmeric
1.25ml/¼ tsp hot chilli powder
75g/3oz creamed coconut
900ml/1½ pints/3¾ cups hot chicken stock
30ml/2 tbsp lemon or lime juice
30ml/2 tbsp crunchy peanut butter
50g/2oz/1 cup thread egg noodles, broken into small pieces
15ml/1 tbsp spring onions, finely chopped
15ml/1 tbsp chopped fresh coriander
salt and black pepper
30ml/2 tbsp desiccated coconut and ½ fresh red chilli, seeded and finely chopped, to garnish

1 Heat the oil in a large pan and fry the garlic for 1 minute until lightly golden. Add the chicken and spices and stir-fry for a further 3–4 minutes.

2 Crumble the creamed coconut into the hot chicken stock and stir until dissolved. Pour on to the chicken and add the lemon juice, peanut butter and egg noodles.

3 Cover and simmer for about 15 minutes. Add the spring onions and fresh coriander, then season well and cook for a further 5 minutes.

4 Meanwhile, place the coconut and chilli in a small frying pan and heat for 2–3 minutes, stirring frequently, until the coconut is lightly browned.

5 Serve the soup in bowls sprinkled with the fried coconut and chilli.

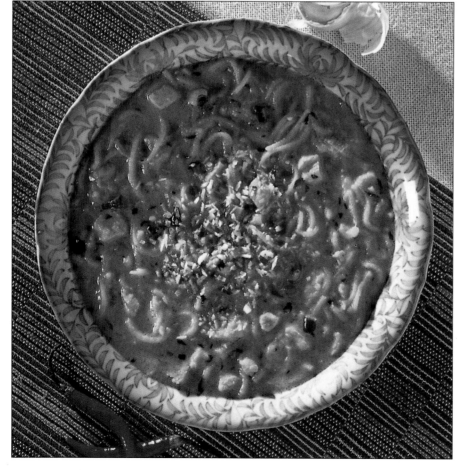

Mussel Bisque

Served hot, this makes a delicious and very filling soup, perfect for a light, lunch-time meal. It is also excellent cold.

INGREDIENTS

Serves 6

675g/1½lb fresh mussels in their shells
150ml/¼ pint/⅔ cup dry white wine or cider
25g/1oz/2 tbsp butter
1 small red onion, chopped
1 small leek, thinly sliced
1 carrot, finely diced
2 tomatoes, skinned, seeded and chopped
2 garlic cloves, crushed
15ml/1 tbsp chopped fresh parsley
15ml/1 tbsp chopped fresh basil
1 celery stick, finely sliced
½ red pepper, seeded and chopped
250ml/8fl oz/1 cup whipping cream
salt and black pepper

1 Scrub the mussels and pull off the beards. Discard any broken ones, or any that don't close when tapped. Place them in a large pan with half the wine and 150ml/¼ pint/⅔ cup water.

2 Cover and cook the mussels over a high heat until they open up. (Discard any which don't open.) Transfer the mussels with a draining spoon to another dish and leave until cool enough to handle. Remove the mussels from their shells; leaving a few in their shells, to garnish if you like.

3 Strain the stock through a piece of muslin or a fine cloth to get rid of any grit. Heat the butter in the same large pan and cook the onion, leek, carrot, tomatoes and garlic over a high heat for 2–3 minutes.

4 Reduce the heat and cook for a further 2–3 minutes, then add the cooking liquid, 300ml/½ pint/1¼ cups water and the herbs and simmer for a further 10 minutes. Add the mussels, celery, peppers, cream, and seasoning to taste. Serve hot.

Tomato and Blue Cheese Soup

INGREDIENTS

Serves 4

1.5kg/3lb ripe tomatoes, peeled, quartered, and seeded
2 garlic cloves, finely chopped
30ml/2 tbsp vegetable oil
1 leek, chopped
1 litre/1¾ pints/4 cups unsalted chicken stock
115g/4oz blue cheese, cut into smallish pieces
45ml/3 tbsp single cream
a few fresh basil leaves, plus extra for garnishing
175g/6oz bacon, cooked and crumbled
salt and black pepper

1 Preheat the oven to 200°C/400°F/ Gas 6. Spread the tomatoes in a shallow baking dish with the garlic.

2 Add seasoning to taste and bake for about 35 minutes.

3 Heat the oil in a large saucepan. Add the leek and carrot and season lightly with salt and pepper. Cook over a low heat for 10 minutes, stirring occasionally, until softened.

4 Stir in the stock and tomatoes. Bring to the boil, then lower the heat, cover and simmer for 20 minutes.

5 Add the blue cheese, cream and basil. Transfer to a food processor or blender and process until smooth, working in batches if neccessary. Taste and adjust the seasoning.

6 Reheat the soup, but do not boil. Ladle into bowls and garnish with the crumbled bacon and basil.

Corn and Crab Chowder

Chowder comes from the French word *chaudron* meaning a large cooking pot. This is what the fishermen on the east coast of the United States used for boiling up whatever was left over from their catch for supper.

INGREDIENTS

Serves 4

25g/1oz/2 tbsp butter
1 small onion, chopped
340g/12oz can sweetcorn, drained
600ml/1 pint/2½ cups milk
175g/6oz can white crabmeat, drained
115g/4oz/1 cup peeled, cooked
   prawns
2 spring onions, finely chopped
150ml/¼ pint/⅔ cup single cream
pinch of cayenne pepper
salt and black pepper
4 whole prawns in shells, to garnish

1 Melt the butter in a large saucepan and gently fry the onion for 4–5 minutes, until softened.

2 Reserve 30ml/2 tbsp of the sweetcorn for the garnish and add the remainder to the pan with the milk. Bring the soup to the boil, then reduce the heat, cover the pan and simmer over a low heat for 5 minutes.

3 Pour the soup, in several batches if necessary, into a blender or food processor and whizz until smooth.

4 Return the soup to the pan and stir in the crabmeat, prawns, spring onions, cream and cayenne pepper. Reheat gently over a low heat.

5 Meanwhile, place the reserved corn kernels in a small frying pan without oil and dry-fry over a medium heat until golden and toasted.

6 Season the soup well and serve each bowlful topped with a few of the toasted kernels and a whole prawn.

Pea and Ham Broth

INGREDIENTS

Serves 4

450g/1lb/2½ cups dried green or
  yellow split peas
1.85 litres/3¼ pints/8 cups water
1 ham bone with some meat left on it,
  or 1 ham hock
1 onion, finely chopped
1 leek, sliced
2 celery sticks, finely sliced
a few fresh parsley sprigs
6 black peppercorns
2 bay leaves
salt
flat leaf parsley, to garnish

1 Rinse the split peas under cold running water. Place the peas in a large pan and add water to cover. Bring to the boil and boil for 2 minutes. Remove the pan from the heat and leave to soak for 1 hour. Drain.

2 Return the peas to the pan and add the measured water, ham bone or hock, onion, leeks, celery, a couple of sprigs of parsley, salt, peppercorns and bay leaves. Bring to the boil, then reduce the heat, cover and simmer gently for 1–1½ hours, until the peas are tender. Skim occasionally.

3 Remove the bay leaves and the ham bone or hock from the soup. Cut the meat off the bone, discarding any fat and chop the meat into small cubes. Set the meat aside. Discard the ham bone and the bay leaves.

4 Purée the soup in batches in a food processor or blender. Pour into a clean saucepan and add the chopped ham. Check the seasoning. Simmer the soup for 3–4 minutes to heat through before serving. Garnish with parsley.

Turkey and Lentil Soup

INGREDIENTS

Serves 4
25g/1oz/2 tbsp butter or margarine
1 large carrot, chopped
1 onion, chopped
1 leek, white part only, chopped
1 celery stick, chopped
115g/4oz mushrooms, chopped
45ml/3 tbsp dry white wine
1 litre/1¾ pints/4 cups chicken stock
10ml/2 tsp dried thyme
1 bay leaf
115g/4oz/½ cup brown or green
   lentils
225g/8oz cooked turkey, diced
salt and black pepper

1 Melt the butter or margarine in a large saucepan. Add the carrot, onion, leek, celery and mushrooms. Cook for 3–5 minutes, until softened.

2 Stir in the wine and chicken stock. Bring to the boil and skim off any foam that rises to the surface. Add the thyme and bay leaf. Reduce the heat, cover, and simmer for 30 minutes.

3 Add the lentils and continue cooking, covered, for 30–40 minutes more, until they are just tender. Stir the soup from time to time.

4 Stir in the diced turkey and season to taste with salt and pepper. Cook until just heated through. Ladle the soup into bowls and serve hot.

COLD STARTERS

Chilled starters are often thought of as summer food, though they make a light and refreshing start to a meal at any time of the year. Fruity combinations such as Minted Melon Salad, or Parma Ham with Mango are especially good to serve before a rich main course. While fish dishes, such as Potted Shrimps, and Smoked Haddock Pâté are best followed by lighter foods. Leeks, served cold with a mustard dressing, or marinated in a walnut dressing, make a delicious change in winter, and goat's cheese, either marinated or grilled is good with almost anything.

Egg and Tomato Salad with Crab

INGREDIENTS

Serves 4

1 round lettuce
2 x 200g/7oz cans crabmeat, drained
4 hard-boiled eggs, sliced
16 cherry tomatoes, halved
½ green pepper, seeded and
    thinly sliced
6 stoned black olives, sliced

For the dressing

250ml/8fl oz/1 cup mayonnaise
10ml/2 tsp fresh lemon juice
45ml/3 tbsp chilli sauce
½ green pepper, seeded and finely
    chopped
5ml/1 tsp prepared horseradish
5ml/1 tsp Worcestershire sauce

1 To make the dressing, place all the ingredients in a bowl and mix well Set aside in a cool place.

2 Line four plates with the lettuce leaves. Mound the crabmeat in the centre. Arrange the eggs around the outside with the tomatoes on top.

3 Spoon some of the dressing over the crabmeat. Arrange the green pepper slices on top and sprinkle with the olives. Serve immediately with the remaining dressing.

Summer Tuna Salad

This colourful salad is perfect for a summer lunch in the garden – use canned or freshly cooked salmon in place of the tuna, if you like.

INGREDIENTS

Serves 4–6

175g/6oz radishes
1 cucumber
3 celery sticks
1 yellow pepper
175g/6oz cherry tomatoes, halved
4 spring onions, thinly sliced
45ml/3 tbsp fresh lemon juice
45ml/3 tbsp olive oil
2 x 200g/7oz cans tuna, drained and
    flaked
30ml/2 tbsp chopped fresh parsley
salt and black pepper
lettuce leaves, to serve
thin strips twisted lemon rind,
    to garnish

1 Cut the radishes, cucumber, celery and yellow pepper into small cubes. Place in a large, shallow dish with the cherry tomatoes and spring onions.

2 In a small bowl, stir together the salt and lemon juice with a fork until dissolved. Pour this over the vegetable mixture. Add the oil and pepper to taste. Stir to coat the vegetables. Cover and set aside for 1 hour.

3 Add the flaked tuna and parsley to the mixture and toss gently until well combined.

4 Arrange the lettuce leaves on a platter and spoon the salad into the centre. Garnish with the lemon rind.

VARIATION

Prepare the vegetables as above and add the parsley. Arrange lettuce leaves on individual plates and divide the vegetable mixture among them. Place a mound of tuna on top of each and finish with a dollop of mayonnaise.

Leek Terrine with Deli Meats

This attractive starter is very simple to make yet looks spectacular. You can make the terrine a day ahead and keep it covered in the refrigerator. If your guests are vegetarian offer chunks of feta cheese.

INGREDIENTS

Serves 6

20–24 small young leeks
about 225g/8oz mixed sliced meats, such as Parma ham, coppa or pancetta
50g/2oz/²⁄₃ cup walnuts, toasted and chopped
60ml/4 tbsp walnut oil
60ml/4 tbsp olive oil
30ml/2 tbsp white wine vinegar
5ml/1 tsp wholegrain mustard
salt and black pepper

1 Cut off the roots and most of the green part from the leeks. Wash them thoroughly under cold running water to get rid of any grit or mud.

2 Bring a large pan of salted water to the boil. Add the leeks, bring the water back to the boil, then reduce the heat and simmer for 6–8 minutes, until the leeks are just tender. Drain well.

3 Fill a 450g/1lb loaf tin with the leeks, placing them alternately head to tail and sprinkling each layer as you go with salt and pepper.

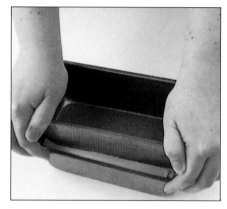

4 Put another loaf tin inside the first and gently press down on the leeks. Carefully invert both tins and let any water drain out.

5 Place one or two weights on top of the tins and chill the terrine for at least 4 hours, or overnight.

6 Meanwhile, make the dressing. Whisk together the walnut and olive oils, vinegar and wholegrain mustard in a small bowl. Add seasoning to taste.

7 Carefully turn out the terrine on to a board and cut into slices using a large sharp knife. Lay the slices of leek terrine on serving plates and arrange the slices of meat alongside.

8 Spoon the dressing over the slices of terrine and scatter over the chopped walnuts. Serve at once.

COOK'S TIP

For this terrine, it is important to use tender young leeks. The white part mainly is used in this recipe, but the green tops can be used in soups. The terrine must be pressed for at least 4 hours – this makes it easier to carve into slices. You can vary the sliced meats as you like. Try, for example, bresaola, salami, smoked venison or roast ham.

VARIATION

If you are short of time, serve the cooked leeks simply marinated in the walnut and mustard dressing.

Avocado and Papaya Salad

INGREDIENTS

Serves 4

2 ripe avocados
1 ripe papaya
1 large orange
1 small red onion
25–50g/1–2oz small rocket leaves or
  lamb's lettuce

For the dressing

60ml/4 tbsp olive oil
30ml/2 tbsp fresh lemon or lime juice
salt and black pepper

1 Halve the avocados and remove the stones. Carefully peel off the skin, then cut each avocado half lengthways into thick slices.

2 Peel the papaya. Cut it in half lengthways and scoop out the seeds with a spoon. Set aside 5ml/1 tsp of the seeds for the dressing. Cut each papaya half lengthways into eight slices.

3 Peel the orange. Using a small sharp knife, cut out the segments, cutting either side of the dividing membranes. Cut the onion into very thin slices and separate into rings.

4 Combine the dressing ingredients in a small bowl and mix well. Stir in the reserved papaya seeds.

5 Assemble the salad on four individual serving plates. Alternate slices of papaya and avocado. Add the orange segments and a small mound of rocket topped with onion rings. Spoon over the dressing.

Asparagus with Creamy Vinaigrette

INGREDIENTS

Serves 4

675g/1½lb asparagus spears
30ml/2 tbsp raspberry vinegar
2.5ml/½ tsp salt
5ml/1 tsp Dijon mustard
75ml/5 tbsp sunflower oil
30ml/2 tbsp soured cream or natural
  yogurt
white pepper
175g/6oz fresh raspberries

1 Fill a large shallow saucepan with water – it needs to be about 10cm/4in deep. Bring to the boil.

2 Trim off the tough ends from the asparagus spears. You may need to remove 2.5–5cm/1–2in from each spear.

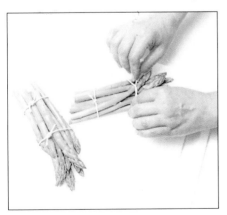

3 Tie the asparagus spears into two bundles. Lower the bundles into the boiling water and cook for 5–7 minutes, until just tender.

4 Carefully remove the asparagus bundles from the boiling water and immediately immerse them in cold water to prevent further cooking. Drain and untie the bundles. Pat dry the spears with kitchen paper. Chill the asparagus for at least 1 hour.

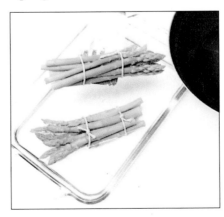

5 Place the vinegar and salt in a bowl and stir with a fork until the salt is dissolved. Stir in the mustard, then gradually whisk in the oil until blended. Add the soured cream or yogurt and pepper to taste.

6 To serve arrange the asparagus spears on individual plates and drizzle the dressing across the middle of the spears. Garnish with the fresh raspberries and serve at once.

Minted Melon Salad

This starter is nicest made with two different kinds of melon; choose from an orange-fleshed Charentais or Cantaloupe, a pale green Galia or Ogen, or a small white-fleshed Honeydew.

INGREDIENTS

Serves 4
2 ripe melons

For the dressing
30ml/2 tbsp roughly chopped fresh mint
5ml/1 tsp caster sugar
30ml/2 tbsp raspberry vinegar
90ml/6 tbsp extra virgin olive oil
salt and black pepper
mint sprigs, to decorate

1 Halve the melons, then scoop out the seeds using a dessertspoon. Cut the melons into thin wedges using a large sharp knife and remove the skins.

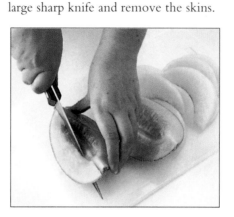

2 Arrange the two different varieties of melon wedges alternately on four individual serving plates.

3 To make the dressing, whisk together the mint, sugar, vinegar, oil and seasoning in a small bowl, or put in a screw-top jar and shake until blended.

4 Spoon the mint dressing over the melon wedges and decorate with mint sprigs. Serve very lightly chilled.

Marinated Goat's Cheese with Herbs

These little cheeses are delicious spread on toasted slices of French bread, brushed with olive oil and rubbed with garlic.

INGREDIENTS

Makes 6
6 individual fresh soft goat's cheeses
90ml/6 tbsp chopped fresh mixed parsley, thyme and oregano
2 garlic cloves, chopped
12 black peppercorns, lightly crushed
150ml/¼ pint/⅔ cup extra virgin olive oil
salad leaves, to serve

--- COOK'S TIP ---
Any herbs can be added to the marinade – try chervil, tarragon, chives and basil. If you prefer, reserve the herb-flavoured oil, and use it to make a salad dressing.

1 Arrange the individual fresh goat's cheeses in a single layer in a large shallow non-metallic dish.

2 Put the chopped herbs, garlic and crushed peppercorns in a blender or food processor. Start the machine, then pour in the oil and process until the mixture is fairly smooth.

3 Spoon the herb mixture over the cheeses, then cover and leave to marinate in the fridge for 24 hours, basting the cheeses occasionally.

4 Remove the cheeses from the fridge about 30 minutes before serving and allow them to come back to room temperature. Serve the cheeses on a bed of salad leaves and spoon over a little of the olive oil and herb mixture.

Pears and Stilton

Stilton is the classic British blue cheese, but you could use another flavourful cheese such as blue Cheshire or Gorgonzola.

INGREDIENTS

Serves 4
4 ripe pears, lightly chilled
75g/3oz blue Stilton cheese
50g/2oz medium fat soft cheese
black pepper
watercress sprigs, to garnish

For the dressing
45ml/3 tbsp light olive oil
15ml/1 tbsp lemon juice
10ml/½ tbsp toasted poppy seeds
salt and pepper

1 First make the dressing; place the olive oil, lemon juice, poppy seeds and seasoning in a screw-topped jar and shake together until emulsified.

2 Cut the pears in half lengthways, then scoop out the cores and cut away the calyx from the rounded end.

3 Beat together the Stilton, soft cheese and a little pepper. Divide this mixture among the cavities in the pears.

4 Shake the dressing to mix it again, then spoon it over the pears. Serve garnished with watercress.

Potted Shrimps

The tiny brown shrimps traditionally used for potting are very fiddly to peel. Since they are rare nowadays, it is easier to use peeled, cooked shrimps instead.

INGREDIENTS

Serves 4
225g/8oz shelled shrimps
225g/8oz/1 cup butter
pinch of ground mace
salt
cayenne pepper
dill sprigs, to garnish
lemon wedges and thin slices of brown
   bread and butter, to serve

1 Chop a quarter of the shrimps. Melt 115g/4oz/½ cup of the butter slowly, carefully skimming off any foam that rises to the surface.

2 Stir all the shrimps, the mace, salt and cayenne into the pan and heat gently without boiling. Pour the shrimps and butter mixture into four individual pots and leave to cool.

3 Heat the remaining butter in a clean small saucepan, then carefully spoon the clear butter over the shrimps, leaving behind the sediment.

4 Leave until the butter is almost set, then place a dill sprig in the centre of each pot. Leave to set completely, then cover and chill.

5 Transfer the shrimps to room temperature 30 minutes before serving with lemon wedges and thin slices of brown bread and butter.

Melon and Crab Salad

INGREDIENTS

Serves 6

450g/1lb fresh crabmeat
120ml/4fl oz/½ cup mayonnaise
45ml/3 tbsp soured cream or
   natural yogurt
30ml/2 tbsp olive oil
30ml/2 tbsp fresh lemon or
   lime juice
2–3 spring onions, finely chopped
30ml/2 tbsp finely chopped fresh
   coriander
1.25ml/¼ tsp cayenne pepper
salt and black pepper
1½ cantaloupe or small honeydew
   melons
3 medium chicory heads
fresh coriander sprigs, to garnish

1 Pick over the crabmeat very carefully, removing any bits of shell or cartilage. Leave the pieces of crabmeat as large as possible.

2 In a medium-sized bowl, combine all the other ingredients except the melons and chicory, and mix well. Fold the crabmeat into this dressing.

3 Halve the melons and remove and discard the seeds. Cut them into thin slices, then remove the rind.

4 Arrange the salad on six individual serving plates, making a decorative design with the melon slices and whole chicory leaves. Place a mound of dressed crabmeat on each plate and garnish the salads with fresh coriander sprigs.

Smoked Trout Salad

Horseradish is as good a partner to smoked trout as it is to roast beef. In this recipe it combines with yogurt to make a delicious light salad dressing.

INGREDIENTS

Serves 4
1 oakleaf or other red lettuce
225g/8oz small tomatoes, cut into
  thin wedges
½ cucumber, peeled and thinly sliced
4 smoked trout fillets, about
  200g/7oz each, skinned and flaked

For the dressing
pinch of English mustard powder
15–20ml/3–4 tsp white wine vinegar
30ml/2 tbsp light olive oil
100ml/3½fl oz/scant ½ cup
  natural yogurt
about 30ml/2 tbsp grated fresh or
  bottled horseradish
pinch of caster sugar

1 First, make the dressing. Mix together the mustard powder and vinegar, then gradually whisk in the oil, yogurt, horseradish and sugar. Set aside for 30 minutes.

COOK'S TIP

Salt should not be necessary in this recipe because of the saltiness of the trout.

2 Place the lettuce leaves in a large bowl. Stir the dressing again, then pour half of it over the leaves and toss lightly using two spoons.

3 Arrange the lettuce on four individual plates with the tomatoes, cucumber and trout. Spoon over the remaining dressing and serve at once.

Melon and Grapefruit Cocktail

This pretty, colourful starter can be made in minutes, so it is perfect for when you don't have time to cook, but want something really special to eat.

INGREDIENTS 🍎

Serves 4

1 small Galia or Ogen melon
1 small Charentais melon
2 pink grapefruit
45ml/3 tbsp orange juice
60ml/4 tbsp red vermouth
seeds from ½ pomegranate
mint sprigs, to decorate

COOK'S TIP

To check if the melons are ripe, smell them – they should have a heady aroma, and give slightly when pressed gently at the stalk end.

---

1 Halve the melons lengthways and scoop out all the seeds. Cut into wedges and remove the skins, then cut across into large bite-sized pieces.

2 Using a small sharp knife, cut the peel and pith from the grapefruit. Holding the fruit over a bowl to catch the juice, cut between the grapefruit membranes to release the segments. Set aside the grapefruit segments.

3 Stir the orange juice and vermouth into the reserved grapefruit juice.

4 Arrange the melon pieces and grapefruit segments haphazardly on four individual serving plates. Spoon over the dressing, then scatter with the pomegranate seeds. Decorate with mint sprigs and serve at once.

Parma Ham with Mango

Other fresh, colourful fruits, such as figs, papaya or melon would go equally well with the Parma ham in this light, elegant starter. It is amazingly simple to prepare and can be made in advance – ideal if you are serving a complicated main course.

INGREDIENTS 🍎

Serves 4

12 slices Parma ham
1 ripe mango
black pepper
flat leaf parsley sprigs, to garnish

1 Separate the Parma ham slices and arrange four on each of four individual plates, crumpling the ham slightly to give a decorative effect.

2 Cut the mango into three thick slices around the stone, then slice the flesh and discard the stone. Neatly cut away the skin from each slice.

3 Arrange the mango slices in among the ham. Grind over some black pepper and serve garnished with flat leaf parsley sprigs.

Feta Tabbouleh in Radicchio Cups

The radicchio cups are simply a presentation idea. If you prefer, spoon the bulgur wheat mixture on to a serving plate lined with cos lettuce leaves.

INGREDIENTS

Serves 4

75g/3oz/generous ⅓ cup bulgur wheat
60ml/4 tbsp olive oil
juice of 1 lemon, or more to taste
4 spring onions, chopped
90ml/6 tbsp chopped flat leaf parsley
45ml/3 tbsp chopped fresh mint
2 tomatoes, peeled, seeded and diced
175g/6oz feta cheese, cubed
salt and black pepper
1 head radicchio
flat leaf parsley sprigs, to garnish

1 Soak the bulgur wheat in cold water for 1 hour. Drain thoroughly in a sieve and press out the excess water.

2 Mix together the oil, lemon juice and seasoning in a bowl. Add the bulgur wheat, then mix well, making sure all the grains are coated with the dressing. Leave at room temperature for about 15 minutes so the bulgur wheat can absorb some of the flavours.

3 Stir in the spring onions, parsley, mint, tomatoes and feta. Taste and adjust the seasoning, adding more lemon juice to sharpen the flavour, if necessary.

4 Separate out the leaves from the radicchio and select the best cup-shaped ones. Spoon a little of the tabbouleh into each one. Arrange on individual plates or on a serving platter and garnish with flat leaf parsley sprigs.

Bresaola, Onion and Rocket Salad

INGREDIENTS

Serves 4

2 medium onions, peeled
75–90ml/5–6 tbsp olive oil
juice of 1 lemon
12 thin slices bresaola
50–75g/2–3oz rocket
salt and black pepper

1 Slice each onion into eight wedges through the root.

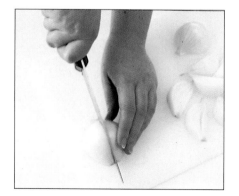

2 Arrange the onion wedges in a single layer on a grill rack or in a flameproof dish. Brush them with a little of the olive oil and season well with salt and pepper to taste.

3 Place the onion wedges under a hot grill and cook for about 8–10 minutes, turning once, until they are just beginning to soften and turn golden brown at the edges.

4 Meanwhile, to make the dressing, mix together the lemon juice and 60ml/4 tbsp of the olive oil in a small bowl. Add salt and black pepper to taste and whisk well until the dressing is thoroughly blended.

5 If you have grilled the onions on a grill rack, then transfer them to a shallow dish once they are cooked.

6 Pour the lemon dressing over the hot onions and leave until cold.

7 When the onions are cold, arrange the bresaola slices on individual serving plates with the onions and rocket. Spoon over any remaining dressing and serve at once.

Leeks with Mustard Dressing

Pencil-slim baby leeks are increasingly available, and are beautifully tender. Use three or four of these smaller leeks per serving.

INGREDIENTS

Serves 4
8 slim leeks, each about 13cm/5in long
5–10ml/1–2 tsp Dijon mustard
10ml/2 tsp white wine vinegar
1 hard boiled egg, halved lengthways
75ml/5 tbsp light olive oil
10ml/2 tsp chopped fresh parsley
salt and black pepper

1 Steam the leeks over a pan of boiling water until just tender.

2 Meanwhile, stir together the mustard and vinegar in a bowl. Scoop the egg yolk into the bowl and mash thoroughly into the vinegar mixture using a fork.

3 Gradually work in the oil to make a smooth sauce, then season to taste.

4 Lift the leeks out of the steamer and place on several layers of kitchen paper, then cover the leeks with several more layers of kitchen paper and pat dry.

5 Transfer the leeks to a serving dish while still warm, spoon the dressing over them and leave to cool. Finely chop the egg white using a large sharp knife, then mix with the chopped fresh parsley and scatter over the leeks. Chill until ready to serve.

COOK'S TIP

Although this dish is served cold, make sure that the leeks are still warm when you pour over the dressing so that they will absorb the mustardy flavours.

Smoked Haddock Pâté

Arbroath smokies are small haddock that are deheaded and gutted but not split before being salted and hot-smoked.

INGREDIENTS

Serves 6

3 large Arbroath smokies, about 225g/
  8oz each
275g/10oz/1¼ cups medium fat soft
  cheese
3 eggs, beaten
30–45ml/2–3 tbsp lemon juice
pepper
sprigs of chervil, to garnish
lemon wedges and lettuce leaves,
  to serve

1 Preheat the oven to 160°C/325°F/ Gas 3. Butter six ramekin dishes.

2 Lay the smokies in a baking dish and heat through in the oven for 10 minutes. Carefully remove the skin and bones from the smokies, then flake the flesh into a bowl.

COOK'S TIP

There should be no need to add salt to this recipe, as smoked haddock is naturally salty – taste the mixture to check.

3 Mash the fish with a fork and work in the cheese, then the eggs. Add lemon juice and pepper to taste.

4 Divide the fish mixture among the ramekins and place in a roasting tin. Pour hot water into the roasting tin to come halfway up the dishes. Bake for 30 minutes, until just set.

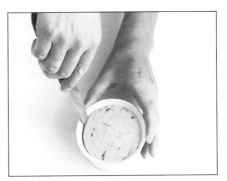

5 Allow to cool for 2–3 minutes, then run a knife around each dish and invert on to a warmed plate. Garnish with chervil sprigs and serve with the lemon and lettuce.

French Goat's Cheese Salad

INGREDIENTS

Serves 4

200g/7oz bag prepared mixed salad
   leaves
4 rashers back bacon
16 thin slices French bread
115g/4oz full fat goat's cheese

For the dressing

60ml/4 tbsp olive oil
15ml/1 tbsp tarragon vinegar
10ml/2 tsp walnut oil
5ml/1 tsp Dijon mustard
5ml/1 tsp wholegrain mustard

1 Preheat the grill to a medium heat.
Rinse and dry the salad leaves, then
arrange in four individual bowls. Place
the ingredients for the dressing in a
screw-topped jar, shake together well
and reserve.

2 Lay the bacon rashers on a board,
then stretch with the back of a knife
and cut each into four. Roll each piece
up and grill for about 2–3 minutes.

3 Meanwhile, slice the goat's cheese
into eight and halve each slice. Top
each slice of bread with a piece of
goat's cheese and pop under the grill.
Turn over the bacon and continue
cooking with the goat's cheese toasts
until the cheese is golden and bubbling.

4 Arrange the bacon rolls and toasts
on top of the prepared salad leaves,
shake the dressing well and pour a little
of the dressing over each one.

— COOK'S TIP —

If you prefer, just slice the goat's cheese
and place on toasted French bread. Or use
wholewheat toast for a nutty flavour.

Greek Salad Pittas

Horiatiki is the Greek name for
this classic salad made with feta
– a cheese made from ewes' milk.
Try serving it in hot pitta breads
with a minty yogurt dressing.

INGREDIENTS

Makes 4

115g/4oz/1 cup diced feta cheese
¼ cucumber, peeled and diced
8 cherry tomatoes, quartered
½ small green pepper, seeded and
   thinly sliced
¼ small onion, thinly sliced
8 black olives, stoned and halved
30ml/2 tbsp olive oil
5ml/1 tsp dried oregano
4 large pitta breads
60ml/4 tbsp natural yogurt
5ml/1 tsp dried mint
salt and black pepper
fresh mint, to garnish

1 Place the cheese, cucumber, tomatoes, pepper, onion and olives in a
bowl. Stir in the olive oil and oregano,
then season well and reserve.

2 Place the pitta breads in a toaster or
under a preheated grill for about 2
minutes, until puffed up. Meanwhile,
to make the dressing, mix the yogurt
with the mint, season well and reserve.

3 Holding the hot pittas in a tea
towel, slice each one from top to
bottom down one of the longest sides
and open out to form a pocket.

4 Divide the prepared salad among
the pitta breads and drizzle over a
spoonful of the dressing. Serve the
pittas immediately, garnished with the
fresh mint.

HOT STARTERS

In cooler weather, hot starters come into their own, and crumbly, creamy shellfish gratins, Devilled Kidneys, and Baked Eggs with Tarragon are all traditional winter fare. A few dishes, such as Herb Omelette with Tomato Salad, are even substantial enough to make a light lunch-time meal. However hot starters aren't necessarily rich and filling; lighter, contemporary recipes such as mini kebabs made with mussels and scallops, Spinach Salad with Bacon and Prawns, and Hot Tomato and Mozzarella Salad are perfect before a filling main course.

Creamy Creole Crab

INGREDIENTS

Serves 6

2 x 200g/7oz cans crabmeat
3 hard boiled eggs
5ml/1 tsp Dijon mustard
75g/3oz/6 tbsp butter or margarine, at
  room temperature
1.25ml/¼ tsp cayenne pepper
45ml/3 tbsp sherry
30ml/2 tbsp chopped fresh parsley
120ml/4fl oz/½ cup single or whipping
  cream
2–3 thinly sliced spring onions,
  including some of the green parts
50g/2oz/½ cup dried white breadcrumbs
salt and black pepper

1 Preheat the oven to 180°C/350°F/ Gas 4. Flake the crabmeat into a medium-size bowl, keeping the pieces of crab as large as possible and removing any shell or cartilage.

2 In a medium-size bowl, crumble the egg yolks with a fork. Add the mustard, 60ml/4 tbsp of the butter or margarine and the cayenne pepper, then mash together to form a paste. Mix in the sherry and parsley.

3 Chop the egg whites and mix in with the cream and spring onions. Stir in the crabmeat and season well.

4 Divide the crab mixture equally among six greased scallop shells or individual baking dishes. Sprinkle with the breadcrumbs and dot with the remaining butter or margarine.

5 Bake for about 20 minutes, until bubbling hot and golden brown.

Scallop and Mussel Kebabs

INGREDIENTS

Serves 4

65g/2½oz/5 tbsp butter, at room
  temperature
30ml/2 tbsp finely chopped fresh fennel
  fronds or parsley
15ml/1 tbsp fresh lemon juice
32 small scallops
24 large mussels in the shell
8 bacon rashers
115g/4oz/1 cup fresh white
  breadcrumbs
45ml/3 tbsp olive oil
salt and black pepper
parsley sprigs and lemon peel,
  to garnish
hot toast, to serve

1 Make the flavoured butter by com-
bining the butter with the chopped
herbs, lemon juice and salt and pepper
to taste. Mix well, then set aside.

2 In a small saucepan, cook the scallops in their own liquid for about
5 minutes, or until just tender. (If there
is no scallop liquid – retained from the
shells after shucking – use a little fish
stock or white wine.) Drain and pat
dry with kitchen paper.

3 Scrub the mussels well, discarding
any broken ones, and rinse under
cold running water. Place in a large
saucepan with about 2.5cm/1in of
water. Cover the pan and steam the
mussels over a medium heat until they
open. Remove them from their shells,
and pat dry on kitchen paper. Discard
any mussels that have not opened.

4 Thread four scallops, three mussels
and a rasher of bacon on to eight
15cm/6in wooden or metal skewers,
weaving the bacon between the scallops and mussels.

5 Preheat the grill. Spread out the
breadcrumbs on a plate. Brush the
seafood with olive oil and roll in the
crumbs to coat all over.

6 Place the skewers on the grill
rack. Grill for 4–5 minutes on each
side until crisp and lightly browned.
Serve immediately garnished with the
parsley sprigs and lemon peel and
accompanied by hot toast and the
flavoured butter.

Goat's Cheese Tarts

INGREDIENTS

Serves 6

6–8 sheets filo pastry (about
   115g/4oz)
50g/2oz/4 tbsp butter, melted
350g/12oz firm goat's cheese
9 cherry tomatoes, quartered
120ml/4fl oz/½ cup milk
2 eggs
30ml/2 tbsp single cream
large pinch of white pepper

--- COOK'S TIP ---

Keep the filo pastry under a damp cloth
while working to prevent the sheets from
drying out.

1 First, preheat the oven to 190°C/
375°F/Gas 5.

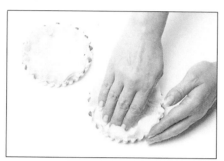

2 Grease six 10cm/4in tartlet tins.
Then for each tin, cut out four
rounds of filo pastry, each about
11.5cm/4½in in diameter. Place one
round in the tin and brush with butter.
Top with another filo round and
continue until there are four layers of
filo; do not butter the last layer. Repeat
for the remaining tins.

3 Place the pastry-lined tins on a
baking sheet. Cut the goat's cheese
log into six slices and place a slice of
cheese in each of the pastry cases.

4 Arrange the tomato quarters
around the goat's cheese slices.

5 Place the milk, eggs, cream and
pepper in a measuring jug or bowl
and whisk to mix. Pour into the pastry
cases, filling them almost to the top.

6 Bake in the oven for 30–40
minutes, until puffed and golden.
Serve hot or warm, with a mixed
green salad if desired.

Baked Eggs with Tarragon

Traditional *cocotte* dishes or small ramekins can be used, as either will take one egg perfectly.

INGREDIENTS

Serves 4

40g/1½oz/3 tbsp butter
120ml/4fl oz/½ cup double cream
15–30ml/1–2 tbsp chopped fresh
     tarragon
4 eggs
salt and black pepper
fresh tarragon sprigs, to garnish

1 Preheat the oven to 180°C/350°F/ Gas 4. Lightly butter four small ovenproof dishes, then warm them in the oven for a few minutes.

2 Meanwhile, gently warm the cream. Sprinkle some tarragon into each dish, then spoon in a little of the cream.

3 Carefully break an egg into each of the prepared ovenproof dishes, season the eggs with salt and pepper and spoon a little more of the cream over each of the eggs.

4 Add a knob of butter to each dish and place them in a roasting tin containing sufficient water to come halfway up the sides of the dishes. Bake for 8–10 minutes, until the whites are just set and the yolks still soft. Serve hot, garnished with tarragon sprigs.

Herb Omelette with Tomato Salad

This is ideal as a snack or a light lunch – use flavourful, fresh plum tomatoes in season.

INGREDIENTS

Serves 4
4 eggs, beaten
30ml/2 tbsp chopped, mixed fresh
  herbs, such as chives, marjoram,
  thyme or parsley, or 10ml/2 tsp dried
knob of butter
45–60ml/3–4 tbsp olive oil
15ml/1 tbsp fresh orange juice
5ml/1 tsp red wine vinegar
5ml/1 tsp grainy mustard
2 large beef tomatoes, thinly sliced
salt and black pepper
fresh herb sprigs, to garnish

1 Beat the eggs, herbs and seasoning together. Heat the butter and a little of the oil in an omelette pan.

2 When the fats are just sizzling, pour in the egg mixture and leave to set, stirring very occasionally with a fork. This omelette needs to be almost cooked through (about 5 minutes).

3 Meanwhile, heat the rest of the oil in a small pan with the orange juice, vinegar and mustard, and add salt and pepper to taste.

4 Roll up the cooked omelette and neatly cut into 1cm/½ in wide strips. Keep them rolled up and transfer immediately to the hot plates.

5 Arrange the sliced tomatoes on the plates with the omelette rolls and pour on the warm dressing. Garnish with herb sprigs and serve at once.

Three-cheese Croûtes

INGREDIENTS

Serves 2–4
4 thick slices of slightly stale bread
a little butter, or mustard
75g/3oz Brie
45ml/3 tbsp fromage frais
50g/2oz grated Parmesan or mature
  Cheddar
1 small garlic clove, crushed
salt and black pepper
black olives, to garnish

COOK'S TIP

If you have Brie which will not ripen fully, this is an excellent way of using it up. You'll need a knife and fork to eat this tasty starter.

1 Preheat the oven to 200°C/400°F/ Gas 6. Place the bread slices on a baking sheet, close together, and spread with either butter or mustard.

2 Cut the Brie into thin slices or pieces and arrange the slices or pieces evenly on the bread.

3 Mix together the fromage frais, Parmesan or Cheddar, garlic, and seasoning to taste. Spread over the Brie and the bread to the corners.

4 Bake for 10–15 minutes, or until golden and bubbling. Serve immediately, garnished with black olives.

Spinach Salad with Bacon and Prawns

Serve this hot salad with plenty of crusty bread for mopping up the delicious juices.

INGREDIENTS

Serves 4

105ml/7 tbsp olive oil
30ml/2 tbsp sherry vinegar
2 garlic cloves, finely chopped
5ml/1 tsp Dijon mustard
12 cooked king prawns
115g/4oz streaky bacon, rinded and cut into strips
about 115g/4oz fresh young spinach leaves
½ head oak leaf lettuce, roughly torn
salt and black pepper

1 To make the dressing, whisk together 90ml/6 tbsp of the olive oil with the vinegar, garlic, mustard and seasoning in a small pan. Heat gently until thickened slightly, then keep warm.

2 Carefully peel the prawns, leaving the tails intact. Set aside.

3 Heat the remaining oil in a frying pan and fry the bacon until golden and crisp, stirring occasionally. Add the prawns and stir-fry for a few minutes until warmed through.

4 While the bacon and prawns are cooking, arrange the spinach and torn oak leaf lettuce leaves on four individual serving plates.

5 Spoon the bacon and prawns on to the leaves, then pour over the hot dressing. Serve at once.

—— COOK'S TIP ——

Sherry vinegar lends its pungent flavour to this delicious salad. You can buy it from large supermarkets and delicatessens.

Mussels with Cream and Parsley

INGREDIENTS

Serves 2

675g/1½lb mussels in the shell
½ fennel bulb, finely chopped
1 shallot, finely chopped
45ml/3 tbsp dry white wine
45ml/3 tbsp single cream
30ml/2 tbsp chopped fresh parsley
freshly ground black pepper

1 Scrub the mussels under cold running water. Remove any barnacles with a small knife and tear away the beards. Rinse once more.

2 Place the mussels in a large wide pan with a lid. Sprinkle them with the fennel, shallot and wine. Cover and place over a medium-high heat shaking the pan occasionally. Steam for 3–5 minutes, until the mussels open.

3 Lift out the mussels with a slotted spoon and remove the top shells. Discard any that did not open. Arrange the mussels, on their bottom shells, in one layer in a shallow serving dish. Cover and keep warm in a low oven.

4 Place a double layer of dampened muslin or a clean tea towel in a sieve set over a bowl. Strain the mussel cooking liquid through the muslin or tea towel. Return the liquid to a clean saucepan and bring to the boil.

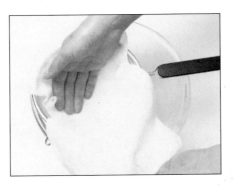

5 Add the cream, stir well and boil for 3 minutes to reduce slightly, then stir in the parsley. Spoon the sauce over the mussels and sprinkle with freshly ground black pepper. Serve the mussels immediately.

Cheese and Spinach Puffs

INGREDIENTS

Serves 6

150g/5oz/1 cup cooked, chopped
   spinach
175g/6oz/¾ cup cottage cheese
5ml/1 tsp ground nutmeg
2 egg whites
30ml/2 tbsp grated Parmesan cheese
salt and black pepper

1 Preheat the oven to 220°C/425°F
Gas 7. Brush six ramekins with oil.

2 Mix together the spinach and cottage cheese in a small bowl, then
add the nutmeg and seasoning to taste.

3 Whisk the egg whites in a separate
bowl until stiff enough to hold soft
peaks. Fold them evenly into the
spinach mixture using a spatula or
large metal spoon, then spoon the
mixture into the oiled ramekins,
dividing it evenly, and smooth the tops.

4 Sprinkle with the Parmesan and
place on a baking sheet. Bake for
15–20 minutes, or until puffed and
golden brown. Serve immediately.

COOK'S TIP

Make sure that the spinach is not too wet.
Tip it into a sieve and press firmly with
the back of a wooden spoon to squeeze
out the excess liquid.

Lemony Stuffed Courgettes

INGREDIENTS

Serves 4

4 courgettes, about 175g/6oz each
5ml/1 tsp sunflower oil
1 garlic clove, crushed
5ml/1 tsp ground lemongrass
finely grated rind and juice of ½ lemon
115g/4oz cooked long-grain rice
175g/6oz cherry tomatoes, halved
30ml/2 tbsp toasted cashews
salt and black pepper
sprigs of thyme, to garnish

COOK'S TIP

Other cooked grains would be equally
good in this dish, try bulgur wheat, cous-
cous or wholegrain rice.

1 Preheat the oven to 200°C/400°F/
Gas 6. Halve the courgettes lengthways and use a teaspoon to scoop out
the centres. Blanch the shells in boiling
water for 1 minute, then drain well.

2 Chop the courgette flesh finely and
place in a saucepan with the oil and
garlic. Stir over moderate heat until
softened, but not browned.

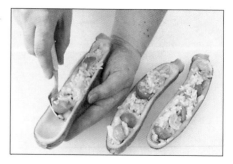

3 Stir in the lemongrass, lemon rind
and juice, rice, tomatoes, and
cashews. Season well and spoon into
the courgette shells. Place the shells in
a baking tin and cover with foil.

4 Bake for 25–30 minutes or until
the courgettes are tender, then
serve hot, garnished with thyme sprigs.

Chinese Garlic Mushrooms

Tofu is high in protein and very low in fat, so it is a very useful food to keep handy and it makes a tasty stuffing for mushrooms.

INGREDIENTS 🍎

Serves 4

8 large open cup mushrooms
3 spring onions, sliced
1 garlic clove, crushed
30ml/2 tbsp oyster sauce
285g/10oz packet marinated tofu, cut into small dice
200g/7oz can sweetcorn, drained
10ml/2 tsp sesame oil
salt and black pepper

1 Preheat the oven to 200°C/400°F/ Gas 6. Finely chop the mushroom stalks and mix with the spring onions, garlic, and oyster sauce.

2 Stir in the diced marinated tofu and sweetcorn, season well with salt and pepper, then carefully spoon the filling into the mushrooms.

3 Brush the edges of the mushrooms with the sesame oil. Arrange the stuffed mushrooms in a baking dish and bake for 12–15 minutes, until the mushrooms are just tender, then serve at once.

— COOK'S TIP —

If you prefer, omit the oyster sauce and use light soy sauce instead.

Devilled Kidneys

'Devilled' dishes are always hot and spicy. If you have time, mix the spicy ingredients together in advance to give the flavours time to mingle and mature.

INGREDIENTS

Serves 4

10ml/2 tsp Worcestershire sauce
15ml/1 tbsp prepared English mustard
15ml/1 tbsp lemon juice
15ml/1 tbsp tomato purée
pinch of cayenne pepper
40g/1½oz/3 tbsp butter
1 shallot, finely chopped
8 lambs' kidneys, skinned, halved
 and cored
salt and black pepper
15ml/1 tbsp chopped fresh parsley,
 to garnish

1 Mix the Worcestershire sauce, mustard, lemon juice, tomato purée, cayenne pepper and salt together to make a sauce.

2 Melt the butter in a frying pan, add the shallot and cook, stirring occasionally, until softened but not coloured.

— COOK'S TIP —

To remove the cores from the kidneys, use kitchen scissors, rather than a knife – you will find that it is much easier.

3 Stir the kidney halves into the shallot in the pan and cook over a medium-high heat for about 3 minutes on each side.

4 Pour the sauce over the kidneys and quickly stir so they are evenly coated. Serve immediately, sprinkled with chopped parsley.

Hot Tomato and Mozzarella Salad

A quick, easy starter with a Mediterranean flavour. It can be prepared in advance, chilled, then grilled just before serving.

INGREDIENTS

Serves 4
450g/1lb plum tomatoes, sliced
225g/8oz mozzarella cheese, sliced
1 red onion, finely chopped
4–6 pieces sun-dried tomatoes in oil, drained and chopped
60ml/4 tbsp olive oil
5ml/1 tsp red wine vinegar
2.5ml/½ tsp Dijon mustard
60ml/4 tbsp chopped fresh mixed herbs, such as basil, parsley, oregano and chives
salt and black pepper
fresh herb sprigs, to garnish (optional)

1 Arrange the sliced tomatoes and mozzarella in circles in four individual shallow flameproof dishes.

2 Scatter over the chopped onion and sun-dried tomatoes.

3 Whisk together the olive oil, vinegar, mustard, chopped herbs and seasoning. Pour over the salads.

4 Place the salads under a hot grill for 4–5 minutes, until the mozzarella starts to melt. Grind over plenty of black pepper and serve garnished with fresh herb sprigs, if liked.

Asparagus with Tarragon Butter

Eating fresh asparagus with your fingers can be messy, but it is the only proper way to eat it!

INGREDIENTS

Serves 4
500g/1¼lb fresh asparagus
115g/4oz/½ cup butter
30ml/2 tbsp chopped fresh tarragon
15ml/1 tbsp chopped fresh parsley
grated rind of ½ lemon
15ml/1 tbsp lemon juice
salt and black pepper

— COOK'S TIP —
When buying fresh asparagus, choose spears which are plump and have a good even colour with tightly budded tips.

1 Trim the woody ends from the asparagus spears, then tie them into four equal bundles.

2 Place the bundles of asparagus in a large frying pan with about 2.5cm/1in boiling water. Cover and cook for about 6–8 minutes, until the asparagus is tender but still firm. Drain well and discard the strings.

3 Meanwhile, melt the butter in a small pan. Add the tarragon, parsley, lemon rind and juice and seasoning.

4 Arrange the asparagus spears on four warmed serving plates. Pour the hot tarragon butter over the asparagus and serve at once.

INDEX